"When You Come Wearing Slippers is an outstanding resource for planning a life-changing women's retreat. In preparing this comprehensive leader's guide, author Cheris Gaston has given a great gift to the local church. It is a practical, user-friendly tool that has the breath of God upon the pages. As Cheris' pastor, I can also speak for her authentic, passionate love for ministry—she is an incredible servant with a heart for others to experience the joy of Jesus. As God's Word says, 'How beautiful are the feet of those who bring good news' in Romans 10:15."

Dr. Danny Sinquefield, Pastor
Faith Baptist Church, Bartlett, Tennessee

"After working alongside Cheris as one of her pastors, I know her heart. This ladies' retreat guide will enable every church, regardless of size, to have their own ladies' conference. The guide will give your ladies a step-by-step, easy-to-follow process to facilitate their giftedness to result in a kingdom impact. Your ladies will never be the same."

David Smith, Associate Pastor, Education
Faith Baptist Church, Bartlett, Tennessee

"I love this woman! She is a woman after God's own heart. She loves Jesus and loves to encourage others to do the same. God has gifted her greatly. It is obvious that God inspired her to write this. It is so uplifting and detailed. You will be blessed…I know I was!"

Mrs. Kristina Kirkpatrick, Women's Ministry
Faith Baptist Church, Bartlett, Tennessee

When You Come Wearing

Slippers...

When You Come Wearing

Slippers...

The Retreat/Conference Leaders Guide

Cheris Gaston

TATE PUBLISHING & *Enterprises*

Published by Tate Publishing & Enterprises, LLC
127 E. Trade Center Terrace | Mustang, Oklahoma 73064 USA
1.888.361.9473 | www.tatepublishing.com

Tate Publishing is committed to excellence in the publishing industry. The company reflects the philosophy established by the founders, based on Psalms 68:11,
"The Lord gave the word and great was the company of those who published it."

Book design copyright © 2007 by Tate Publishing, LLC. All rights reserved.
Cover design by Jennifer L. Redden
Interior design by Kristen Polson
Illustrations by Bonnie Orange

Published in the United States of America

ISBN: 978-1-6024700-9-5
07.06.29

To all of my precious sisters in Christ!
(You have richly blessed my life with the presence of your lives in mine).

Acknowledgments

I would like to thank my best friend and precious husband, Danny, for the many hours he helped me with "computer details" and for his never-failing love and encouragement throughout this project and always!

I am grateful to my dear parents for being my "cheering section" and believing in me no matter what. (Example: I remember when I was that quiet, shy, and fearful child in the third grade who forgot every note of her piano recital piece except middle "C" on the night of her recital. Thank you, Mom, for the undeserved standing ovation). Who ever knew that so many words would pour into a book from an adult who was once that child? Thank you, Momma and Daddy, for being there at the beginning to show me what true unconditional love was in all things and for pointing me in the direction of our wonderful Lord.

As I grew older and stronger in my faith, I grew in God-focused courage and in my love for God. With my eyes on the Lord, I have stepped out in His strength to make the dream of this book become a reality. So I thank you, dear Lord, above all!

Also, I thank my precious children, Hannah and Seth, whose presence in my life constantly remind me of how very grateful I should be to our gracious Heavenly Father who sits on His throne each day—waiting for me to *come and rest at His feet!*

Table of Contents

Introduction

Why did I write a retreat book for leaders entitled, *When You Come Wearing Slippers...*? I will tell you what I know, but God had the writing of it planned long before I did.

For years, I have firmly believed that God can speak to people in a powerful way through retreats. While in college, I went to a retreat that had a wonderful impact on my life, and I remember longing for a deeper relationship with the Lord because of it. Being older now, I still feel that there is a need for everyone, especially Christians, to participate in a retreat when given the opportunity. Retreats can give one the chance to break away from everyday responsibilities and reflect on the greatness of God. In a retreat, all of the material is not packed into one brief hour; it is experienced in many hours, where each hour of material can build on the previous one (I've helped lead in 3 retreats and have written material for 2 of them).

As an adult woman, I have wondered why retreat books designed for women are not more available in the Christian bookstores. It puzzled me as to why there weren't many people who were willing to sit down and compile a complete retreat package for leaders and participants, including the subject material for the retreat. God had begun to work on my heart to get me ready for the task He had planned for me. I decided that one day I would like to write a complete "from-beginning-to-end" retreat book to help a small group of ladies from a church be able to plan and lead a women's retreat for their own church. (The women of a church shouldn't have to wait for a guest speaker from another church to lead them through an in-depth study or seminar when God has blessed women in each church with some God-given gifts that make them capable to lead their own retreat).

One spring afternoon when I was on my way to pick up my daughter from school, God put His plan into action. He gave me so many ideas about being "at His feet" and serving "as His feet" that I couldn't get home fast enough to write them down on paper. And ever since then, whenever I sat down to work on this book, I knew He would provide me with whatever I needed to make this dream become a reality!

For a while, I put the completion of this book "on hold." During that time, I struggled with the fact that I was not letting His Will be accomplished through me. But once I decided to finish the book, the ideas were flowing again just as before. Then, I really knew that I was doing what He called me to do. He confirmed that I was serving Him in the way that I was supposed to serve, and that confirmation brought a great sense of peace. I now had total commitment to this project.

So, now you hold in your hands the book that I feel has been in God's hands all along. God was my first Editor! Just as God helped me to write and edit, He will help you to lead. God knows who can lead or who has the potential to lead at each church, and you fall into one of those categories. He is very pleased that you decided to "step forward" and serve Him. As I looked to Him for guidance, so should you.

If your focus is on God the entire time, then, you and 4 other ladies with the same focus can successfully plan and lead this retreat from beginning to end with the information I give you in this book. It was my goal to write a book where there was enough material and/or resources provided for each leader, in order that she could take the necessary steps to fulfill her responsibilities for the retreat. Then, as all of the leaders combined their hard work and efforts, they could produce a very exciting retreat for the ladies of their local church. This book will answer all of the "who," "what," "where," "when," and "why's" of the retreat.

Since I feel so strongly about the importance of one's relationship to God, and one's responsibility as a Christian to serve others, I feel passionate about the material in this book. Hopefully, that passion comes across in my writing and in my own life. This retreat book is packed with a large amount of exciting material, such as: games, skits, study sessions, decoration ideas, promotional ideas, dinner options, itinerary, and so much more! You'll also be given detailed instructions on how to plan before the retreat and how to lead at the retreat.

Why is the retreat called, *When You Come Wearing Slippers...*? That's an easy one to answer. When you come wearing slippers, you are willing to rest in Him and "step" into the next pair of shoes when your heart is ready. The "foot" represents who you are, while the shoe represents what you will "do."

As a leader of the retreat, get ready to stretch, grow, learn, serve, and have fun in the process! This will be a memorable weekend for the ladies of your church, and you have a wonderful opportunity to help make it happen! It doesn't matter if the retreat is for ten ladies or two hundred or more because the material is important and can be scaled down or up to fit the needs of how many are coming. The important thing to remember is that they're coming, and you have the opportunity to be used by God to help them grow spiritually. So, pray before you start running around to fulfill your obligations, then, listen as He leads. Why? Some serious serving is about to take place.

Your first set of instructions is to turn to the "Table of Contents," and find the page number for the section written for your leadership role. As you flip to your section, this incredible journey through footwear will begin.

Serving in His Behalf,
Cheris

Retreat Itinerary

Listing responsible leader and time estimates

Friday

Responsible Leader	Event	Comments	Time estimates
Promotional leader	Get your "foot book" *	Check in and get materials	20 min.
Guests	Complete the "Foot Fun" sheet *	Sit with someone and do the worksheet together	10 min.
Retreat leader	"Hello, 'slipper-wearing' feet"	Welcome/prayer	5 min.
Food/decorations	"Sole food"	Dinner	30-45 min.
Retreat leader	"Meet other Feet"	Game	15 min.
Retreat leader	"Your shoes may change"	Overview	5 min.
Music leader/ keepsake maker	"Foot Soak"	Refreshing music	10 min.
Retreat speaker	"At His Feet" *	Study session	20-30 min.
Promotional Leader	"To Be or Not To Be"	Modern skit of Mary and Martha	5 min.
Retreat leader	"A Foot Gathering" *	Small groups	20-30 min.
Retreat leader	"Time out in this foot race"	Break	15 min.
Music leader/ keepsake maker	"Toe-tappin' time"	Sing-a-Long	10 min.
Retreat speaker	"As His Feet" *	Study session	20-30 min.
Retreat leader	"Get Ready, Get Set, and Serve"	Game	15-20 min.
Promotional leader	"Socks"	Skit	5 min.
Retreat leader	"Feet facts"	Closing remarks and instructions to prayer partners worksheet	5 min.
Guests	"Find a pair of socks" *	Prayer partners	15 min.
Food/decorations	"Foot loose"	Fun, food, and fellowship	10+min
Guests	"Before you rest your feet" *	Mix-and-Match sheet	5 min.

Saturday

Responsible Leader	Event	Comments	Time estimates
Guests	"Time to be at His feet" *	Devotional	15 min.
Food/decorations	"Fuel the feet"	Breakfast	20-30 min.
Guests	"Fun with friends" *	Worksheet	5 min.
Retreat leader	"Foot stretch"	Exercises	5 min.
Music leader/ keepsake maker	"In honor of His feet"	More than music	15-20min.
Retreat leader	"Feet of Faith" exercise	A mysterious adventure	20-30 min.
Retreat leader/ Music leader/ keepsake maker	"Feet of Faith" coming together *	Worksheet/sharing/ passing out of keepsakes	30 min.
Retreat speaker	"Because of the Master's Feet" *	Study session	20-30 min.
Retreat speaker/ Music leader/ keepsake maker	"Time for Him"	Challenge/music/ sharing	15+min.
Retreat leader	"Farewell, feet"	Closing/Thank you's/ Prayer	5-10 min.

* These items are located in *When You Come Wearing Slippers: The Retreat Participant's Guide*

Chairperson/Retreat Leader

"Big Toe"

(Responsibilities, retreat material, and checklist)

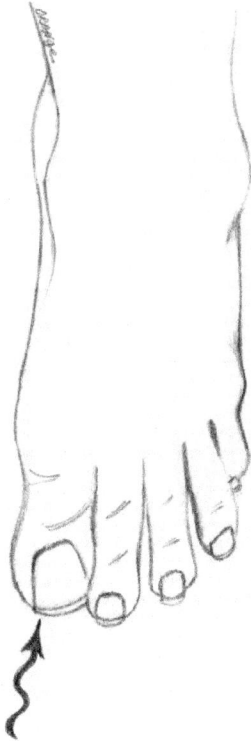

Chairperson responsibilities that begin at least seven-eight weeks before the retreat:

More than likely, you're the one who saw a need for a women's retreat. If so, you are sensitive to the needs of the women of your church, and you desire that the women of your church grow closer to their Lord and to each other. If someone handed you this retreat book, then he/she feels that you possess the leadership qualities to make this retreat a successful and worthwhile event. In either case, the Lord had a part in your selection, and that alone should encourage you to give 100% to an opportunity that can make stronger warriors out of the women who walk through your church halls.

This section will fully equip you to get ready for the retreat. (If there are not many women in your church who will "step up" to assume, a leadership role in the retreat, the Lord may place it in your heart to serve as the retreat speaker. If this is the case, know that with the Lord's help, this book will allow you to "fill those shoes" as well). So, let's begin looking at your responsibilities.

The first thing you should do as chairperson is pray! Start with praying for yourself. To start an adventure like this one, you need to be saturated in prayer. After praying, you will be ready to make wise decisions in the planning of the retreat that will result in a "prayer-powered" retreat. His Spirit will lead you and keep you persevering when problems arise. Keep focused on your goals so that complications will not deter you from accomplishing those goals.

You also need to pray before you select the rest of the leaders. Ask the Lord to specifically put people's names in your mind that will fill the other leadership responsibilities. In finding leaders, it might be helpful to think of women who display the qualities that are mentioned in "Choosing Leaders" which are provided for you next.

Choosing leaders

"Footprint artist" (Promotion and skits) You might want to select a "people" person or someone who can exhibit a lot of enthusiasm for a special event like this one. Because this is a leadership position, she should also be a good Christian role model. Her work is to get people excited about coming, and then once she gets them there, give them lasting impressions of the retreat by having skits from this book presented. Her responsibilities involve vigorous promotion and turning skits on paper into performances on stage.

Remember that this leader must be dependable and respected. Doing her job well is very important because if she can't get women motivated to come, then sadly, there will not be a retreat. Pray for her daily that she can persevere until her work is done. Remind her that everything she does for the retreat is an example of service to the Lord.

"Fancy footwork-er" (Food and decorations). This particular leader will provide the footwork that will feed the tummies and will hold the attention of the eyes for a moment with her handiwork. She is responsible for food organization and decorations not associated with the worship area. Not only does she need to be a good Christian role model, but she also needs to be a strong organizer with a willing, servant's heart. Pray that her hands and feet will not grow tired, but that she will enjoy doing for her sisters in Christ. Also, pray that she knows that her preparations will complement the spiritual food that the women will be receiving from the other leaders.

"Toe tapper" (Music leader and "keepsake" maker). Find

someone who is somewhat musically inclined and is sensitive to the needs of the women of your church. She doesn't have to be the best singer in the choir, but she does have to know how to "tap the women's toes," meaning, get their attention. She needs to be one who can lead, make musical selections, and have a loving relationship with the Lord. This leader will create the mood for the sessions, and the condition of her heart is more important than the sound of her voice. Pray that she will ask for God's guidance in her selection of music and in ways to involve people as she shares that music.

"Foot specialist" (Speaker/study leader.) Your speaker should be knowledgeable of God's Word and have a true desire to share in a way that will motivate and encourage others into action. This woman will have a lot of material to cover and will need to have teaching and/or speaking capabilities. It should be obvious by the way she lives her life that she truly strives to be "at Christ's feet" and strives to serve "as His feet" whenever He calls her to do so.

After you pray, God will reveal their names to you. Once He does, go quickly to each woman, and share that God brought her name to you to help as a leader in the retreat. Pray with each of them. When you hear four of them say, "Yes," press on!

Pray for the retreat. Pray that it will have an impact on the ladies who attend as well as the leaders who will give much time and effort in making it happen.

Now that you have your leaders, it's time to schedule a leaders' meeting. Make sure that all of your leaders can attend.

• •

At the meeting:

How to Begin

Begin the meeting "on the right foot" by thanking the leaders for their willingness to serve. Open with prayer, then; welcome them to the first leaders' meeting for the "When You Come Wearing Slippers" retreat.

Leaders' Books

Introduce each leader by her retreat title and tell what her general responsibilities are. Then, pass out the leaders' retreat books so that each leader can get a better understanding of her specific responsibilities and see her resource material in her section of the book.

Date

As leaders are skimming over their pages, talk with the promotion leader about a specific date for the retreat that will allow plenty of time to promote. (Your retreat needs to be at about six weeks after the first promotional item is underway at the church. Calendars are usually clear for women with that much advanced notice.

After deciding on a date, make sure it is a good one for all leaders involved. If not, you'll have to bring up other dates until all leaders are able to attend the retreat. (The book is written for a Friday night and Saturday morning format, but you can amend it to suit your needs).

Location

As a group, brainstorm location ideas for the retreat. Talk about the needs of the women of your church. You may need to use the church building if many of the women work and wouldn't be able to travel somewhere else and be there between 5:30–6:00 p.m. (If you choose a different place, such as a home or a group of cabins, try not to choose a place more than an hour away, since you may lose the interest of some women). In deciding on a place; remember that you'll need a rather large room for everyone to gather for study sessions, skits, music-led times, and small groups. Another room will be needed for meals and fellowship. (Games can be played in the same room where meals are eaten, if it is a large room like a fellowship hall. Otherwise, you will also need a place for games to be played).

Overnight or Not Overnight?

The leaders must also decide on whether or not they want to stay at the retreat place for the entire time, or go home to sleep and come back the next morning. I've been to both, and there are pros and cons to each. The positives for staying at the church/ retreat setting are: 1) you have more time for fellowship, 2) you have a lack of distractions from the "outside world," and 3) you have a real feeling of "retreat" among the ladies. The negatives for staying there are: 1) you have to find a place to sleep for everyone, 2) you have to bring bedding and toiletries, and 3) you will need a place that provides showers. The argument for going home at night is that you don't have the negatives you just listed above. While the sad part of not staying at the retreat place overnight is that you don't have the positives listed above. Contemplate on the possible number of women that might attend so you will know how many. Also, consider the distance from homes to the retreat place. If it's a long distance, you may have some that won't return the following morning if they don't sleepover. Important note: The retreat material could last until 10:30–11:00p.m. Friday night if you decide to break for the evening after the prayer partner segment. What do you think the women of your church would want to do? It may be tough to make a decision, but it's one that has to be made.

Registration Price

You must also talk to the leaders about a fair price to charge the women for the retreat. Consider the cost of books, food-related items, decorations, materials for keepsakes, and rental of lodging/retreat facilities, if applicable (Each leader responsible for these items may need to do some checking of prices before the next meeting.) Come up with a possible price, then decide on a specific price after some of the leaders have done some price checking.

Questions

Next, ask if the leaders have any initial questions that need to be addressed to you or the team of leaders. After questions are answered, as chairperson, offer your assistance in helping with any problems or questions between meetings. Give your phone number and e-mail address, and ask for theirs, if you don't already have them.

Volunteer/ Next Meeting

Encourage leaders to enlist as many volunteers as they need to fulfill the given responsibilities. Tell the leaders that getting people involved is a great way to make sure that people will attend! Encourage them to be enthusiastic when talking to people about the retreat, but do not give away too much information or details concerning the retreat.

Keep others curious, but excited! Finally, schedule to meet with all leaders again in one week.

Participant's Guide

When You Come Wearing Slippers: The Retreat Participant's Guide contains games, worksheets, and a devotional, which will allow each participant to get the most out of this experience. If you would like to purchase a participant guide for each person attending, please contact me at cherisgaston@yahoo. com for further information. Please include "Slippers–Participant's Guide" in your subject line.

. . . .

Second leader's meeting:

Again...

Again, begin with prayer. Then, agree upon a date, a price, a place, and if you haven't already done so, work out any issues that may have arisen during the week. Remind them that you're just a phone call away if they have any questions before the retreat. Continue to generate enthusiasm with your leaders. Participants will only be as enthusiastic as their leaders.

Photographer

Ask the leaders if they know anyone who might be coming to the retreat who might volunteer to be the retreat photographer or "Foot-ographer." She doesn't have to be a professional. She does need to own a camera, know how to use it, and be willing to take enough pictures to help promote enthusiasm for next year's retreat!

Sound Equipment

Discuss with the group about whether or not any sound equipment will be needed at the retreat. If so, you need to contact the person(s) who could arrange it.

Get Promotion Started

Urge the promotional leader to get promotion underway immediately, especially if the retreat is in six weeks or less! Have the promotional leader tell the other leaders when the first Sunday is to register for the retreat, and encourage the leaders to wear slippers to their Sunday school classes and/or after church that morning! Not only is this a fun idea, but it will also be a great way to promote the retreat and unite the leaders as a group of prayer warriors "on foot!"

Close

Pray at the close of the meeting for God's guidance and strength in the coming weeks. Then, send all of your "lead feet" out the door to begin preparing for the retreat, "When You Come Wearing Slippers."

• •

One week before the retreat:

Make calls

Call all leaders to make sure that all plans are running smoothly; if they're not running smoothly, work together to solve any problems. Have them check with their volunteers, if they have any, to make sure everyone will have her work done that needs to be completed before the retreat.

• •

Day of retreat:

Get the retreat place ready

If at all possible, go to your retreat place that morning with as many leaders as you can to begin setting up for the retreat by:

- putting up tables and chairs for meals, putting up a "welcome table" for retreat books and nametags
- putting up decorations
- helping bring in food (if applicable) , depending on the food leader's option
- getting the kitchen ready
- getting in place a stand for the speaker
- helping get sound system ready (if applicable)
- helping bring in props for skits, speaker, and games.

In other words, get as much done as you possibly can before the retreat begins. When you come that evening, you only should have to bring your leaders' book, your participant's book (see Addendum), your Bible, and the other items you've requested the other participants to bring. Remember, you are to enjoy and gain from this retreat too. That's why it's so important to get most of the hard labor done before the retreat begins.

Time to begin the retreat

Wearing slippers, you and the other leaders arrive early at a specific time designated by you. Greet as many participants as you can. Mingle and make everyone feel comfortable. Direct them to the "welcome table" where they can get their participant books and name tags.

Remember that at the retreat, you are the one who takes

care of everyone. First, you need to take care of your leaders, and make sure their needs are met in order that they can lead well. Secondly, you are to make the participants feel at home in this retreat setting. Thirdly, you are the leader of the retreat itself as the "Big toe." You are to make sure that things go as they should and that there is good transition from event to event. As retreat leader, keep a copy of the itinerary close at hand at all times. Many times you are the person who leads interaction between the ladies after they have studied or listened to material. Examples of this are when you lead games or small group sessions.

During the retreat, you need to recognize the leaders the first time they are performing their duties. You don't need to mention them again until the end of the retreat when you are thanking people for their hard work.

When most of the ladies have arrived, give a warm welcome to the group as a whole. An example is provided for you:

Welcome:

Big toe: "Welcome to our retreat this evening! We're so glad that you were able to squeeze this retreat into your busy schedules. But the effort you made in getting here will be well worth it, as you will soon see. We promise that when you leave you won't be the same. That is, 'when you come wearing slippers!'"

"Also, at this time, we need to introduce two of our retreat leaders. We would like to recognize our promotional leader, _____, for getting you here. She is also referred to as our "footprint maker" because she led you here and organized rehearsals for the retreat skits that will make an impression on your heart. And it is our hope that a lasting impression will be made with your life because of your experience this weekend.

In addition, we need to recognize _____, our leader known as the "Fancy footwork-er." She provided the wonderful decorations you see in front of you and took on the monster job of making sure we would be fed well during the entire retreat. We appreciate all of their hard work and the efforts of the rest of our leaders that will be recognized at a later time."

(*Say a prayer for the food and retreat before eating)

*After dinner, you may need to instruct the women that they need to go to another room if the room they are occupying is not big enough for the mixer game they're about to play.

Game: "Meet Other Feet"

(This is a great game because it allows participants to mingle with each other while playing a fun game).

Supplies needed for game: tape, scissors, and pieces of paper with a shoe name on each one. Eighteen different shoe names are provided for you on the next three pages.

Preparation: Xerox the next three pages following the "Rules" as many times as you need so that each participant will receive one shoe name. Cut the names apart. Get enough people to help you tape a shoe name on the back of each participant without her seeing the name on the paper. You will need about one volunteer per 10 participants for the sake of saving time. Remember that your volunteers need to wear one too. You could place the shoe names on the backs of your volunteers.

Rules: Each person is to mingle with the other ladies while asking only questions where the answer is, "yes" or "no." The questions are to help each person figure out which type of shoes she is supposed to be during the game. Example: The question is, "Do you wear my shoes to play football?" The answer is "No." The first person has "ballet slippers" taped to her back.

She can ask one question and be asked a question by the other person. Then, each must find another person to ask another question. You can only ask if you're a certain type of shoes if you've gathered enough information to make a guess. When someone has figured out what pair of shoes she is, she places her shoe name on the front of her. Continue until everyone has figured out her shoe name. If the game begins to take too much time for a few ladies, you can tell the other ladies that they can give a few hints to the remaining "unsolved shoes."

Galoshes	House slippers	Tap shoes
Ballet slippers	Moccasins	Cowboy boots

High-heels

Hiking boots

Flippers

Tennis shoes

Flip-flops

Snow shoes

Sandals	Saddle Oxfords	Pumps
Cleats	Clogs	Penny loafers

*After the game, you need to instruct the ladies to move to the room that you've designated for the study sessions, skits, and music. Once you are there, give your overview of the retreat. An example is given below.

Overview: "Your Shoes May Change"

Big toe: "So, was it difficult or easy to figure out what type of shoes you were in the game we just played? Tonight, if someone met you just as you are, would it be easy or difficult to figure out if you're a Christian by the way you act? During this retreat, it is important to understand that the foot represents who we are, while the shoe represents the actions we take.

"Let us come to the Lord wearing slippers and resting in Him. He can touch our hearts and teach us truths in such a way that it could powerfully affect the way we live the rest of our lives. At this retreat, let us focus on coming to be at His feet and going as His feet. Why? It's because of His feet.

"Be ready to change your shoes whenever He asks. Listen, and pay attention."

*Immediately following your overview, introduce the music leader before she begins.

An example is given next.

Introduction of music leader:

Big toe: "_____ is our music leader, also known as our 'Toe-Tapper.' She holds the capability of being able to 'tap our toes,' which means get the attention of our hearts. She will soothe or uplift our hearts through songs of inspiration and praise. We look forward to this important time with her as our music leader."

*Check your itinerary. Before the speaker begins her first session, introduce her. An example is given below.

Introduction of Speaker:

Big Toe: "We are honored to have _____ as our retreat speaker and Bible study leader. She is also known as our 'foot specialist' since she will be talking about the feet we should have and what they should do as the feet of Christians" (Also, give some background information about her to show why she is capable of being the retreat study session leader, even if it is just to say how much she loves the Lord and how obvious it is by her actions).

*Check your itinerary. After "To Be or Not to Be" skit, you're to direct the large group to form small groups. They are to respond to the skit they just saw and the Biblical story of Mary and Martha in their small groups by doing the worksheet in their retreat guides entitled, "A foot gathering." An example of what to say is given next.

Introduction to small groups:

Big toe: "Now it is time to reflect on what we've heard and seen about being at the feet of Jesus. We need you to break into small groups of four or five then, work the worksheet in your book called, 'A Foot Gathering'. Let your group decide who in your group will 'walk' you through the questions. But everyone is supposed to participate in answering. Let's make small groups now."

*A copy of the worksheet, "A foot gathering," is on the next page.

After the small group session, tell the ladies they have a fif-teen-minute break.

*Check itinerary. After the "As His Feet" study session, get the ladies ready for a fun game involving ways to serve. An example is provided below.

Introduction to game:

Big Toe: "It's tennis shoe time! We're going to move to _____ (room designated for games) "We're going to play a really fun game called, 'Ready, get set, and serve!' This is a fast competitive game, so you'll have to put your 'best foot' forward. We'll have to split into teams. So if your first name starts with a letter between A-H, you sit together on the right side of the room and your team name will be 'the right shoes.' If your first name starts with the letter between I-Z, you sit on the left side of the room, and your team name will be 'the left shoes.' So, right shoes, and left shoes, let's head that way now."

Instructions to game:
"Get Ready, Get Set, And Serve":

Big Toe: "Teams of shoes, I will call out a certain item that could symbolize or help you in an act of service. Then, I will give the name of the item. The first team that finds the item from their purses and places it in my hand first will receive 2 points. If the other team gets the item in my hand in a rea-sonable amount of time before I share the next act of love, that team will receive 1 point. At the end of the game, the team with the most points will win the game. Each team must select one person who will deliver all of the items to me. It is the team members' responsibility to get the items to this par-ticular person as fast as they can."

*Get someone to keep score for both teams.

DESCRIPTION	ITEM
1. Go to prayer meeting and pray for others.	Car keys
2. Comfort someone who is emotionally hurting.	Tissue
3. Teach small children about the love of God and try to keep them safe in an uncertain world.	Safety pin
4. Take good notes as you prepare to teach your Sunday School lesson	Pen or pencil
5. Show Christian love by taking a depressed friend out to lunch.	Restaurant receipt
6. Visit a new mother, and take a baby gift.	Baby lotion or hand lotion
7. Take food to someone who is in need.	A packet of sugar or sugar substitute
8. Share Christ with others.	Bible
9. Comfort someone who is dealing with physical pain.	Band-aid
10. Be a living example of your love of God.	Write your favorite scripture on a piece of paper including the scripture reference.
11. Give to missions in order that others may hear about the love of Christ	A one dollar bill
12. Send a birthday card to someone.	A stamp
13. Call others and invite them to church.	An address book or cell phone
14. Fellowship with others even when it means getting out of your comfort zone.	Switch shoes with a sister in Christ and both of you run up here together holding hands.

Afterwards:

- Applaud for everyone's fun-filled efforts. Hopefully, you got a lot of laughs as a bonus.
- Announce the score for each team.
- Have a small bag of M&M's for each member of the winning team. (M&M's can represent Mary Magdalene, a loving servant of God)

*Check itinerary. After "Socks" skit, get the group ready to find prayer partners. An example is provided below.

Introduction to Prayer Partners

Big toe: "Tonight, we've looked at the importance of being 'at His feet,' serving 'as His feet,' and even how to protect ourselves during service. Prayer is so important. When serving gets difficult, you need not only your prayers, but also, the prayers of a friend.

She can encourage you, pray for you, and even help you from falling away from serving the Lord.

"Before we break tonight, find a prayer partner, and work the prayer partner sheet in your participant's guide. Find a prayer partner that you will feel comfortable meeting on a regular basis, either by phone or in person. Be sure to bring your pair of white socks with you as you do your worksheet on prayer partners.

"After everyone meets with her prayer partner, we'll break for snacks and fellowship. We ask that before you 'rest your feet,' play the Mix-N-Match worksheet this evening. When you wake up in the morning, find your guide, and read the devotional, 'Slip on Your Hiking Boots' by yourself before we meet for breakfast at (time). We will need your bandanas in the morning, so bring them with you."

(*Give any other announcements that may pertain to your retreat, like sleeping arrangements if you are staying overnight at the retreat).

Big toe: "Now that announcements are done, go find a prayer partner. If you don't know who she should be, let the Lord lead you to that person. If the two of you are the only ones standing in the room at the end, it is a certainty that the Lord must want the two of you to be prayer partners."

While saying this is true, it also helps ease the nerves of someone who is not sure who she is supposed to be paired with. It's not a race to find someone, but taking the time to find the one you're supposed to be with.

"Tomorrow, we will focus on the Master's feet! Good night, and don't forget to do your prayer partners worksheet and your homework."

*A worksheet on prayer partners is provided for you on the following page.

Prayer Partners

1. My prayer partner's name is _____.

2. Her phone number is _____.

3. Take a few moments to share with each other about yourselves. (church background, Christian walk, family, interests, etc).

4. Big prayer concerns in my life right now are:
   Take the time to share these with your prayer partner.

5. After she shares her prayer concerns, list them here.

6. After sharing with each other, stop and pray specifically for these concerns. (You pray out loud for her concerns).

7. My prayer concerns related to service are:
   Share these with your partner.

8. After she shares her prayer concerns related to service, list them here:

9. After sharing with each other, stop and pray specifically for these concerns. (You pray out loud for her concerns).

10. Make a commitment to call each other once a week to pray together over the phone.
    Day of week: _____
    Time: _____
    If for some reason, something happens and you will be away at that time, call your partner and schedule a different time for that week only.

11. Write your name on one of the socks and your prayer

partner's name on the other sock. Tie them together in a knot to symbolize your commitment to each other and to remind you that no one can "untie" your bond of prayer and friendship.

Dear prayer partners,

If both of you stay committed to this time of prayer, it is my belief that God will bless you and work mighty wonders through your lives because you're willing to sit 'at His feet' together as friends each week. Be aware that Satan will do whatever he can to keep you from doing this. So no matter what happens, persevere. Even if you have a rough start, know that it is important that you don't let your commitment fade because of inconvenience. In fact, problems might arise, especially the first few times you try to get together. Just know that you can do this!

He will help you. Just put everything at His feet.

From the retreat author,
Cheris

It's Saturday morning! *Check your itinerary. After the ladies have had time to finish breakfast and the "Fun With Friends" worksheet, it's time for "Foot Stretch." An example is provided for you below.

* Have the women move to the large gathering room for study sessions.

Foot Stretch:

Big Toe: "Good morning, and welcome back everyone! We trust that you had a good night's sleep. Now, it's time to wake up our feet and get motivated to stretch and grow. So, let's do some actual stretching. Stand to your feet." (Group responds). "Now, stand on your tiptoes and reach for the sky. Say this after me, 'All things are possible with Christ!'" (Group responds). "Put your feet back on the ground and begin marching in place. Say this after me, 'We're all soldiers in God's army!'" (Group responds). "Stop marching. Lean to the left and stretch your right arm over your right ear and say this after me, 'We will not lean on our own understanding.'" (Group responds). "Then, let's lean to the right and stretch left arm over the left ear and say, 'but we will trust Him and He will make our paths straight.'" (Group responds). "Stand up straight. Cover your eyes with your hands and begin marching. Listen as I speak to you: Even though we don't know where the paths may lead, we will still follow Him." Let the group continue marching for about 10 seconds. Say, "Halt and uncover your eyes. You listened and you followed. Now, it's time to rest again. You may be seated." (As leader, you sit down as the music leader comes forward.)

*Check your itinerary. After the singing, lead the group in the "Feet of Faith" exercise.

(Different options of carrying out this exercise are provided. Select the option you choose to lead and prepare for. Important: Placement of obstacles, if you choose this option, should be done early Saturday morning before breakfast. Try to have breakfast served in an area different than where your obstacles will be located so they will not be seen).

"Feet Of Faith" Exercise:

*Instructions to leader, regardless of what option you choose:

Move the group to just outside a place where there will be freedom to move around the room easily. Break the group back to where they're paired up with their prayer partners. Have one partner blindfold the other partner with the bandana she brought that morning. Give the following instructions to the group.

Big toe: "You are to build trust and faith in your blindfolded partner. For five minutes, you are to guide her around the room." (possibly outside) "Steer her away from all obstacles and people by giving her very specific instructions such as: turn right or left, step over, go around, etc. She will trust you to guide her correctly. With each correct instruction, she will build her faith in you. As you go through this exercise, think about your relationship with the Lord. Do you trust Him completely? Is your faith strong enough to follow wherever He leads?" (Pause.) "Guides, you may take your partners to the unknown."

*After 5 minutes, instruct the partners to switch places. Before they begin the second time, ask the following questions again.

Big toe: "As you go through this exercise, think about your

relationship with the Lord. Do you trust Him completely? Is your faith strong enough to follow wherever He leads?"

(Pause). "Guides, you may lead your partner who leans on you for guidance."

"Feet of Faith" Exercise - Options/preparations

1. Option One- Guides lead the blindfolded partner around a large room.

2. Option Two- Actually put obstacles in the room. Here are some examples:

   a) Place four chairs together with backs touching and a sign that reads, "Wind around each tree in the forest."

   b) Place a small box on the floor with a sign that reads, "Step over the log."

   c) Place a clothesline across part of the room where participants can reach up and feel it from one end to the other. Have a sign that reads, 'Hold on to the safety rope while crossing the bridge."

   d) Set up a small tent and have a small fan that is out of reach and blowing cool air. Place a sign on it that says "Enter a small cave."

   e) Place a piece of paper on the floor that says "Step over the puddle."

   f) Place a sign on a large wall that says "Touch the mountain, and walk along side it until your guide says, 'Stop.'"

   g) Place a rocking chair in the room with a sign that says "Sit in the boat, and cross the seas to unknown territory!"

***This option could be a lot of fun, but it will take some pre-planning in setting up the room. Also, the guides would need to be told to give extremely specific directions, such as: how big of a step to take, how far back a partner should go before sitting, etc. Keep safety a top priority!

3.   Option Three- Have the participants go outside to a very specific area that has already been inspected for safety. The "sighted" people would be given the boundaries.

4.   Option Four Combine two options. For example, if you chose option two for the first round, you might pick option three for the second round so that the first guide would not be aware of everything as a blindfolded participant.

. . . .

*After the "Feet of Faith" exercise:

Have everyone come back to the large gathering room for prayer. From your heart, lead them in a prayer about trusting God and having deep faith and love for Him, causing them to be responsive to His call - even if it's into unknown territory.

Then, have a share time. Have them look at the "Feet of Faith" worksheet in their participant guides. Ask the group if there's a particular question on the page that someone would like to answer out loud and share with the group. Or, perhaps someone would like to share her testimony on how the Lord is dealing with her heart right now.

*Note: The important thing is to not get boxed-in to doing this important time a certain way. Let the Holy Spirit lead you and the group into a real time of intimacy with the Lord and each other.

*The "Feet of Faith" worksheet is provided for you on the following page.

"Feet of Faith"

1. How did you feel at the beginning of the exercise?

2. Was it easier to trust your guide as you spent more time with her? If so, could this also be the case in your relationship with the Lord?

3. a) What was the most difficult part of the exercise?

   b) Were you able to overcome the difficulty and complete the exercise anyway? ("I can do everything through him who gives me strength." Philippians 4:13 NIV)

4. How can you relate this exercise to your relationship with the Lord in the area of trust?

5. Is your faith strong enough to follow wherever or whenever He leads? Do you recognize His voice? ("When he has brought out all his own, he goes on ahead of them, and his sheep follow him because they know his voice." John 10:4 NIV)

***Write your answer to this question in the space provided below. If you feel led to share your answer with the group, feel free to do so. But if you do or don't get the opportunity to share with them, be sure to talk to God about what He has impressed on your heart. The retreat may end soon, but hopefully, a more intimate relationship with the Lord is just beginning.

*The music leader/ "keepsake" maker will be handing out "keepsakes" after you finish leading the group through the "Feet of Faith" worksheet.

Thank You's/ Closing

*Check your itinerary. After the decision/share time that follows "Because of the Master's Feet," thank the leaders once again and anyone else that needs to be thanked for their hard work or contributions. (Be sure to thank the photographer who was not a retreat leader but was a very important volunteer).

Give any closing announcements, if needed. Then, have the group join hands as you lead them in a closing prayer.

*Ideally, you would like for the retreat to end by 12:00 p.m. so the ladies can leave to get their lunch elsewhere; however, if the retreat is not wrapping up by then, don't worry about it. God's agenda is much bigger and more important than our deadlines on paper. Be flexible in responding to His Spirit. He knows the spiritual needs of the women more than anyone else!

Checklist for Chairperson/Retreat retreat leader ("Big toe"):

Before the first leaders' meeting
- ❑ Pray for you and the retreat.
- ❑ Find the other leaders and pray for them.
- ❑ Schedule the first leaders' meeting.
- ❑ Schedule the second leaders' meeting.

First leaders' meeting
- ❑ Pray.
- ❑ Explain the overall theme.
- ❑ Thank the leaders for their willingness to serve.
- ❑ Pass out leaders' books and help them locate each leader's individual section.
- ❑ Talk about date, place, and price of retreat ideas.
- ❑ Talk about whether participants should stay overnight or not.
- ❑ Answer any initial questions.
- ❑ Encourage them to enlist any volunteers to help them if needed.
- ❑ Schedule another meeting a week away.
- ❑ Give your phone number and e-mail address to leaders and ask for theirs if you don't have them.
- ❑ Determine if participant books will be used for the retreat. If so, make contact by e-mail to get ordering information.
- ❑ Pray.

Second leaders' meeting
- ❑ Pray.
- ❑ Decide on date, place, and price of retreat.

- ❑ Decide if participants will stay overnight or not.
- ❑ Address any new questions or problems.
- ❑ Tell leaders to generate enthusiasm to others about the retreat.
- ❑ Ask if they know someone who would be willing to take pictures at the retreat.
- ❑ Decide whether or not the leaders need sound equipment. If so, make the necessary arrangements.
- ❑ Get the promotion leader to begin promotion immediately!
- ❑ Pray.

One week before the retreat

- ❑ Call leaders to see if plans are running smoothly and if pre-retreat work is nearly finished.
- ❑ Call the people whose names were given at the last meeting to find a photographer or "foot-ographer."
- ❑ Make sure all of the *When You Come Wearing Slippers: The Retreat Participant's Guide* copies have arrived.
- ❑ If you're using obstacles and signs in the "Feet of Faith" exercise, gather or make them.
- ❑ Buy M&M's for the winning team in the "Get Ready, Get Set, and Serve" game.

Day of retreat

- ❑ Go to retreat setting to do any needed set-up before the retreat begins.
- ❑ Bring copies of *When You Come Wearing Slippers: The Retreat Participant's Guide*
- ❑ Ask all leaders to be at retreat setting early. You give them a specific time.

Retreat ready

- ☐ Come to the retreat wearing slippers!
- ☐ Greet participants. Steer them to the "welcome" table.
- ☐ Take care of your leaders when they need help.
- ☐ When most of the people have arrived, give welcome. See the welcome provided.
- ☐ Immediately following welcome, give recognition to the promotional leader and the food and decoration leaders. See the example provided.
- ☐ Take the group to a room where the ladies can move around easily. Lead them in the "Meet Other Feet" game.
- ☐ After the game, take the ladies to the large gathering room. Then, give an overview.
- ☐ Before the music leader begins, "Foot Soak," give her introduction. (See example).
- ☐ After "To Be or Not to Be" skit, lead into small group session, "A Foot Gathering." (See example. A worksheet is provided).
- ☐ After "As His Feet" session, move the ladies to a room where the ladies can move around easily. Then, lead "Get Ready, Get Set, and Serve" game. (Introduction, instructions, and game are provided).
- ☐ After "Socks" skit, lead into the prayer partner exercise and give any announcements for the night. (Introduction and worksheet are provided. Some announcements are provided).

Saturday morning at retreat

- ❏ If you're using obstacles and signs in the "Feet of Faith" exercise, put them in the correct place before breakfast. (Hopefully, others won't see you arrange them).
- ❏ "Welcome" and "Foot Stretch"
- ❏ After the singing time, lead the group in "Feet of Faith" exercise.
- ❏ Lead group in answering questions about "Feet of Faith" exercise.
- ❏ After decision/share time that follows "Because of the Master's Feet" session, thank the leaders, photographer, and others.
- ❏ Give any needed announcements.
- ❏ Lead the group in a closing prayer.
- ❏ Clean up retreat area.

After the retreat

- ❏ Go home and rest!
- ❏ Write hand-written thank-you notes to all of your leaders and any volunteers who helped you carry out your responsibilities.

Dear Chairperson/Retreat leader,

Let me assure you that you have been a blessing to many. Thank you for your willingness to serve and your ability to serve well. It took a leader who truly loves God in order to put this retreat in motion and see it through to the end.

Was it hard work? Yes! Was it worth it? Yes, because the ladies had an opportunity to grow closer to their Lord. And hopefully, you had fun in the process. I know God gently stretched you and made you a better leader as you 'walked' through it with Him holding your hand!

> Thank you for serving "as His feet,"
> Cheris, retreat writer

Promotional Leader

"Footprint Artist"

(Responsibilities, retreat material, and checklist)

Promotional leader's responsibilities

If you were selected as the promotional leader, you must be seen as a person who can handle details well, is dependable with important responsibilities, and is one who can motivate others with enthusiasm. The number of people who come to the retreat will partly depend on how well you are able to promote the event.

Pray

Once you've accepted this position, pray that the Lord will help you as you try to fulfill all of your obligations. You, more than any other leader, will have the majority of your work before the retreat begins. Now, look at the "shoes you must fill."

Place

If the leader team has not decided on a place for the retreat in the first leaders' meeting, gather information about possible places to present to the other leaders at the second meeting. Check things at each place such as: the cost, the distance and time to get there, and the size. See if space allowed is enough to facilitate the events for the retreat, including sleeping arrangements if the leaders decide to encourage participants to stay at the retreat setting overnight. The setting needs to have: a large room for large and small group sessions, and a room where meals/desserts can be eaten. You will also need a place where the women can move around easily to play games, especially if the room for meals is not large enough to include a place to play games, such as a fellowship hall. You may want to check with the food leader to see if there is anything in particular that she needs the retreat place to provide in order that she can carry out her responsibilities well.

After gathering your information on several locations, you might want to call the chairperson to discuss the pros and cons of each place. The two of you are in the positions to decide on a first and second choice before the leaders' second meeting. At the meeting, share your top two choices with the leaders and tell why you decided on these particular choices. After thoughtful discussion, choose a place. Make reservations if needed. If a deposit is needed, perhaps you can ask the leaders to go ahead and pay their registration money in order to compensate the deposit fee.

Announcements/Advertisements

After the date, place, price, and other important information are decided upon at the second meeting, such as whether or not the guests will stay at the retreat place overnight, you are ready to begin promoting immediately, as long as you have about six weeks before the retreat begins.

Get an announcement with the important information about the retreat in the church bulletin each week, and put one in your church's correspondence through the mail, if your church has any. Be sure to include: date, place, price, registration details, and the title of the retreat on any announcements. The following is an example of a first-written announcement:

"Ladies, don't miss this! 'When You Come Wearing Slippers' is the title of our exciting women's retreat scheduled for (day,) (month,) (date) at (place). Registration will begin Sunday after the morning worship service in the church hallway outside of the sanctuary. The cost is (price) for (explain what it includes). So, grab a friend and head to the registration table to sign up! The registration deadline is (day,) (month,) and (date). The retreat will be packed with fun, learning, and fellowship!"

Also, make flyers or posters to display in different places, especially bulletin boards and doors, in the church. Think of an eye-catching slogan to put in the center of the flyer using bold letters, then, put the retreat information in the lower right hand corner. Here are some examples of slogans:

1. "When you come wearing slippers..." see what happens next!

2. "Don't wear high-heels, just be ready to climb high hills!"

3. "Come soak your feet in His Word!"

*Be sure to put on the flyer that you're supposed to come wearing slippers!

If your church has a website, be sure and place an announcement there.

Also, when thinking of announcements, don't forget the pulpit! You or a church staff member can promote the retreat during the announcement time during the morning worship service.

Three Skits
(See the next 9 pages)

"Retreat Bound"

This is a promotional skit for a Sunday morning service 4–6 weeks before the retreat.

Six Characters: Four ladies going to the retreat: "#1," "#2," "#3," and "#4," "Hannah" and "Satan"

Props: four Bibles, four poster-board signs on sticks, four pairs of slippers, chair, sign "Satan," and a laundry basket filled with clothes.

Set-up: Four ladies are holding Bibles, wearing slippers, and carrying signs. (The signs are made of poster boards attached to wooden sticks). "# 1's" poster gives the date and time of the retreat. "#2's" poster gives the place of the retreat. "#3's" poster gives the place to register and the cost of the retreat. "#4's" poster gives the title, "When You Come Wearing Slippers,…" "Hannah" is sitting center stage at the top of the steps with "Satan" standing next to her while the ladies are coming down the aisle of the church. The ladies will come up the steps and stand next to "Hannah" on the opposite side of "Satan." "Satan" will be wearing a sign that says, "Satan." The laundry basket filled with clothes will be hidden behind "Hannah's" chair.

"Retreat Bound"-script:

Hannah: (Begins as ladies file up the steps) "Ladies, why in the world are you wearing slippers and carrying signs?

Satan: (Waving index finger) "You don't have time! You need to do a heap of laundry that weekend. It's already piled up a mile high!"

#1: "Hannah, we're going down to the church to promote our women's retreat, "When You Come wearing Slippers" on (date) and (date). Why don't you come?"

Hannah: (Looks at "Satan" with disgust) "Where is the retreat?"

#2: "It's at the (place)."

Satan: "That would be a good weekend to do a little sewing on the side, you know. Besides, you won't have enough gas in your car to get there, anyway."

#2: "We can even arrange for you to catch a ride with someone, if you'd like to go with someone."

Hannah: "What's the cost?"

#3: "It's (price), and you can register at the registration table outside the sanctuary."

Satan: (Shaking head) "You spend that money and you won't be able to buy that super-sizzle steam iron you've had your eye on."

Hannah: "What will you do at the retreat?"

#4: "We're supposed to have a ton of fun with games, skits, food, fellowship, and Bible study. And as you can tell," (looking down at feet) "the emphasis is on feet." (The ladies all tap their toes up and down).

Satan: "You'll probably have to wear outrageously expensive clothes to impress everyone there! Why bother?"

#1: "We're going to wear comfortable clothes all weekend! In fact, we're wearing slippers to the retreat! Just be sure to bring tennis shoes, a pair of old white socks, a bandana, and a hunger to spend more time with God."

Hannah: "Okay, that settles it. You've talked me into it." (Satan stomping feet). "I'm coming and no one" (looking at Satan) "can change my mind!" (Looks back at group) "I'll even help you promote it!"

(Characters 1–3 say one of the following lines sporadically as walking down the steps. Don't make your line sound rehearsed. Some lines can be spoken on top of each other to sound more like a realistic response).

#1: "Great, Hannah!"

#2: "You'll be glad you did!"

#3: "We're going to have so much fun."

#4: (To #3) "I ought to wear these slippers more often, they're really comfortable." (The four ladies pretend to continue talking while they walk down the aisle.)

Hannah: "I need to go register." (Turns toward Satan) "But before I go, I'll have to get some 'clothes-minded' person to do my dirty laundry every weekend, so I'll be free to go to the retreat!" (Hannah goes behind the chair and grabs laundry basket full of clothes and pours them over Satan's head. Then, she puts laundry basket on the floor next to "Satan.") "I'll have more fun than you will!" (Walks off in the direction of the four ladies)

Satan: (Sounding defeated) "Oh, well, today's score is: Satan 0 and God 1! (He puts the laundry back into the basket and takes it with him as he exits.)

"To Be or Not to Be"

(This is a skit to be used at the retreat following the "At His Feet" study session).

Characters: Mary, Martha, and "radio voice"

Props for Mary: Bible, two pairs of slippers

Props for Martha: watch, apron with two pockets, a pair of socks, feather duster, dish cloth, broom, a throw pillow, a chair, a small table, and a radio

Set-up: Mary is sitting on the floor while reading her Bible and wearing slippers. Martha is wearing the apron over her clothes and a pair of socks on her feet. There's a small table with a radio on it. The table is next to a chair with a pillow.

"To Be or Not to Be" script:

Martha: (Looking at watch) "Okay, I've got 8 hours until the Bible study tonight. (Perturbed) "It doesn't look like Mary's going to help me." (Pulls feather duster out of pocket and makes dusting motions on pretend furniture) "Dust the furniture." (Puts duster back into the pocket and pulls dishcloth out of other pocket and starts to "wash" pretend dishes) "Wash the dishes." (Puts dishcloth back into her other pocket and heads to chair to fluff the pillow) "Fluff the pillow" (Gets the broom leaning against a nearby wall as Mary starts to pray) "And sweep." (She sweeps vigorously around Mary. Mary looks up, smiles, and shakes her head. Mary goes back to praying. The "radio voice" off stage makes a static sound like one would hear on the radio). "Well, who left the radio on?" (She goes to turn it off when she hears the story begin and sits down in the chair).

Radio voice: "Today's Bible story is about the home of Mary and Martha. Let's read from Luke 10: 38–42:

> 'As Jesus and his disciples were on their way, he came to a village where a woman named Martha opened her home to him. She had a sister called Mary, who sat at the Lord's feet listening to what he said. But Martha was distracted by all the preparations that had to be made. She came to him and asked, "Lord, don't you care that my sister has left me to do the work by myself? Tell her to help me!"
>
> "Martha, Martha," the Lord answered, "you are worried and upset about many things, but only one thing is needed. Mary has chosen what is better, and it will not be taken away from her." (Martha turns off the radio).

Mary: (Looks up) "Martha, come join me. I'll help you with the housework later."

Martha: (Walking over to Mary) "I guess I shouldn't have been angry with you. Can you forgive me? (Sitting next to Mary)

Mary: "Of course I can. Martha, you have a wonderful heart of service, and you're very organized in so much that you do. The Lord just doesn't want to be left out of your plans. He should come first, then, the rest will fall into place where it needs to."

Martha: "I guess praying and preparing for this Bible study we're going to teach tonight" (Looking up) "is more important than if there's a cobweb on the third blade of my ceiling fan." (They both laugh). "Okay, tell me what Bible story the study's about tonight. As long as it's not about the home of Mary and Martha..."

Mary: "Well, (pause) actually,.."

Martha: "Oh, Mary. I think my feet are gently being stepped on."

Mary: (Pulls another pair of slippers from behind her) "Try these on." (Martha puts on slippers, smiles, then, reaches for Mary's hand. They bow to pray, then, freeze).

"Socks"

(This is a skit to be used after the "As His feet" study session).

Characters:

"C" (chair person) - lady who is sitting in a chair with a large piece of cloth draped over her

"K" (kneeling person) - lady who is kneeling behind the chair and is hidden except that her arms are coming through two holes to act as if they are the arms of "C"

"Speaker" - playing the part of a commercial announcer

Two volunteers to sit on front row and throw sponges

Props: chair, a large piece of dark cloth (like a sheet) with 2 arm holes cut out, a pair of white socks, white gloves, and at least 10 sponges.

Set-up: "C" sits in the chair and puts her hands in her lap. The speaker drapes the large cloth over "C." "K" gets under the large cloth and kneels behind the chair. "K," wearing white gloves, sticks her hands and arms through the side arm holes in the cloth and waves at the audience until the speaker gets in place to read from the script. (The speaker does not have to memorize the script, but she does need to be able to pay attention to the acting that takes place between "C" and "K" so that she will know when to continue with her lines after certain scripted actions).

"Socks" script:

Speaker: "You try to have a servant's heart at all times. But there will be times when you will get tired." (Speaker pauses while "C" yawns as "K" taps "C's" mouth with her right hand). "You walk many a mile" (Speaker pauses as "C" continues to sit, but "steps" in place as "K" swings arms back and forth, as if "C" is walking). "yes, many a mile, while serving the Lord. You might even get a blister because your shoe has rubbed you the wrong way." (Speaker pauses as "C" places her left foot high on her thigh so that "K" can take "C's" shoe off while "C" is looking at that foot).

C: (When the shoe comes off) "Ow," ("C" looks at heel, then, puts her foot down again).

Speaker: "Those blisters can really hurt sometimes. Your head," ("K" taps "C's" head). "may tell you to stop serving." ("K" holds palm flat and vertically straight to the audience) "The pain's not worth it. But what's really happening is that Satan is whispering in your ear." (Speaker pauses while "K" pulls one of "C's" ears).

C: (When ear is pulled) "Ow!"

Speaker: "But we know that anyone who listens to Satan will hurt the cause of Christ. So when Satan hurls his fiery darts at you," (Speaker pauses as 2 people in the front row throw sponges at "C," while "K" tries to swat at the sponges as "C" gives directions to "K".

C: (Gives directions) "Right, left, left, right, left, right..." (Then, "K" takes her arms "in" to get 2 white socks).

Speaker: "As I was saying, when Satan hurls those fiery darts at you, protect those tired, soar feet with the power of white 'prayer socks!'" (Pause as "K's" arms come quickly out of arm holes holding white 'prayer socks.') "When they're not being worn, ("K" begins to tie socks into a knot. Make sure you practice this beforehand). "Tie the prayer socks in a knot to remind you of their unbreakable strength." (Pause until "K" is finished tying).

"Yes, prayer socks can give you the protection you need to sock Satan out of earshot." (Pause as "K" swings knotted socks violently with one hand while "C" wears an angry face. Then, "K" drops the socks in "C's" lap). "When the heat is on, you may need the power of two socks" ("K" holds up 2 fingers) not just one prayer sock." ("C" nods head while "K" holds up index finger). With prayer, you can knock out the punch of Satan's powerful temptations." ("K" starts throwing punches with her fists). Stay tuned as we end this commercial, so you can learn how to get your prayer socks. God gives the gift of prayer socks to protect you from harm and keep you going strong all day long! ("K" makes muscles with her arms as "C" looks at them. "K" points to speaker and begins clapping. The speaker points to "C" and "K" and begins clapping. "K" comes out from under the drape and both "K" and "C" take a bow before exiting).

*Note: It might help the speaker to highlight her lines in one color and the actions of "C" and "K" in another color.

Additional Information

You will need to perform the promotional skit in about two weeks, which should be four weeks before the retreat. (The other two skits will be performed at the retreat).

Run off enough copies of each skit for each character to have a script for her skit. Think of ladies who you think could be characters in the skit. Be positive and enthusiastic as you ask them to play a part in the skits. If someone seems timid in accepting a part, encourage her to accept. Tell her that each is fun and will require only a small amount of memorization.

Schedule two rehearsals for each skit. (All skits should have separate rehearsals from each other if the cast members of each skit consist of different people). Tell each cast member when and where her two rehearsals are scheduled, and what props to bring for her character.

"Helpful Hints" for all rehearsals

1. Pray, so that the rehearsals are in His hands.

2. Make sure all of the props were brought before you start the rehearsal. (If a cast member doesn't bring a prop, make sure that she knows that it has to be at the next rehearsal).

3. Remind the cast that they're doing a good thing for a great cause, so have fun, but stay focused and committed.

4. Be sure you can hear each person well as you stand at a distance from her.

5. Take notes during each run-through, so that you can give them pointers on how to make the next run-through a better one. Share your notes before the next

run-through, and be sure to compliment the good things you noticed too.

6. Don't let anyone turn her back to the audience while speaking.

7. Request "believability" and enthusiasm from each character.

First rehearsal for each skit

Go over the skits at least three times with script and props. If the rehearsal goes well, you might want to try a run-through without scripts at the end of the rehearsal. Either way, tell them that the next rehearsal will be rehearsed without scripts. Tell them when the next rehearsal will be. Before they leave, thank them for helping and be sure to tell them what a good job they're doing.

Second rehearsal for each skit

Go through the skit without scripts. Rehearse until you're comfortable with their next performance being in front of an audience. "Retreat Bound" will be performed in front of a Sunday morning congregation, while "To Be or Not To Be" and "Socks" will be performed in front of the ladies at the retreat. (If your situation allows, you can schedule a dress rehearsal early Sunday morning and do a sound check with microphones, if being used, before the actual performance of "Retreat Bound" later that morning). End this rehearsal with a positive attitude, and be sure each cast member is aware of the place in the service or program she is to be ready to perform the skit. Remind them to be sure to bring their props then, also.

Registration Table

Decide when registration will begin and when the deadline is. Get at least two volunteers to sit at the registration table after each Sunday morning worship service. Make sure your volunteers wear slippers. It will make the occasion more fun! (In fact, you and several retreat leaders or volunteers can wear slippers after church to promote the retreat. Visuals are great reminders! If someone asks why you're wearing slippers, you have the perfect opportunity to promote the retreat).

Your registration sign-up sheet should include four columns with one of the following listings at the top of each column:1) Name, 2) phone number, 3) paid, and 4) check or cash. Have a bag or box of money at the table to make change for registering guests.

Besides the registration sheet and the extra money to make change, you also need to have: any flyer that the food leader wants given to the guests, copies of "What to bring," and a map to the retreat setting if the place is anywhere different than the church building. Suggestions for the "What to Bring" list are listed below, but you will need to make adjustments depending on whether or not they're staying at the retreat setting overnight.

Some important items for the "What to Bring" sheet:

1. Bible

2. Pen or pencil

3. Slippers (Wear them to the retreat!)

4. Tennis shoes

5. Pair of white socks (old pair)

6. Bandana, in your purse

7. Pajamas, if staying overnight

8. Toiletries, if staying overnight

9. Sleeping bag, if needed

10. Pillow, if staying overnight

11. Towel and washcloth, if staying overnight

12. Specific food items, if asked to bring

Be sure to make plenty of copies of all items you intend to give at the registration table.

Registration money

After each registration, make sure your volunteers give you the money. You keep up with the money and distribute to the leaders the amount of money that each requested at the second meeting to take care of her retreat purchases. Record everything you do while handling the money and distributing it, while making sure the chairperson is aware of all that you are doing. Encourage all leaders to save any receipts from their purchases. Talk to the chairperson, if a leader comes to you for additional money so that the burden of making decisions about money distribution doesn't fall completely on you. It is always wise to hold more than one person accountable where money is concerned. In this way, no one will be seen as suspicious if things don't turn out as planned. Talking with someone else before acting is just a "safety net" for you.

Retreat Books

You are in charge of getting the retreat books *When You Come Wearing Slippers: The Retreat Participant's Guide* to the retreat setting. So, keep this in mind when you set a deadline for registration. Give the retreat leader plenty of time to order the retreat guides, and allow time for shipping.

• •

On the day of the retreat

"Welcome" table

Early that day, help with the set-up at the retreat place, if you can. Get "welcome" table and chairs ready so you and other volunteers will be prepared to hand out name tags and retreat guides at the beginning of the retreat.

Before the retreat begins, put on your slippers and go to your station at the welcome table. (Arrive very early since you need to be there before the guests arrive).

As your skit performers come to the table, show them the itinerary, and point out where in the program they will be performing. (By doing this, they will know exactly when to be prepared to move up front with props).

As all guests come to the table, have volunteers direct the guests to do the "Fun Foot" sheet in their participant guides while waiting for everyone to arrive. Then, relax and enjoy the retreat. Your leadership role is completed unless you have a part in either of the two remaining skits.

Promotional leader's checklist:

Between the first and second leaders' meetings
- ❏ Check out possible retreat places, if this is still undecided. (Talk to the food leader to see if she has special requirements for the kitchen area).

Before the retreat
- ❏ Promote! Promote! Promote!
- ❏ Put an announcement in the church bulletin weekly.
- ❏ Put an announcement in the church's mailed information.
- ❏ Put an announcement on the church's website.
- ❏ Have announcements made in church.
- ❏ Make flyers and posters about the retreat, and then hang them in different, well-seen areas of the church building.
- ❏ Have an announcement made from the pulpit.
- ❏ Read the three skits, and find people to play the parts in each skit.
- ❏ Set a date for the promotional skit to be performed.
- ❏ Set up two rehearsal dates for each skit.
- ❏ Tell cast members of the skits about rehearsal dates, times, and places.
- ❏ Tell the cast members what props to bring to the rehearsals and the performance.
- ❏ Make enough copies of the three skits so that each character in a skit has a copy of the skit where she's a cast member.
- ❏ Attend rehearsals and direct with the use of the "helpful hints."

❏ Have the promotional skit performed about four weeks before the retreat.

❏ Make your own "What to Bring" sheet after looking at the suggested needed items in this book. Make plenty of copies of your revised list and place them on the registration table on the first day of registration.

❏ Make copies of a map to the retreat place and attach one to each of the "What to Bring" sheets if the place is anywhere other than the church.

❏ Decide when registration will begin and when the deadline is.

❏ Put the registration table and chairs near the sanctuary.

❏ Get two volunteers to sit at the registration table each Sunday morning after the morning worship service.

❏ Make sign-up sheet(s) for the registration table.

❏ Get cash in case someone needs to make change when registering.

❏ Collect the registration money and distribute the money to leaders according to their previously requested needs to compensate for retreat expenses.

❏ Find volunteers to sit at the "welcome" table at the retreat.

On the day of the retreat

❏ Take the retreat books for participants to the retreat setting and place them on the "welcome" table.

❏ Help with the retreat set-up, if possible.

❏ Retreat ready! Arrive early at the retreat, and come wearing slippers.

❑ While at the "welcome" table, make guests feel welcome as they arrive at the retreat.
❑ Help with the skits, if needed.

After the retreat
❑ Help put the retreat place back in good order.
❑ Go home, and rest!
❑ Write hand-written thank you notes to those who helped fulfill your leader responsibilities.

Dear Promotional leader,

After the "welcome" table you can relax and fully enjoy the retreat. Most of your hard work is completed, unless you're helping with the two remaining skits in some way. Thank you for being willing to serve. Your needed efforts helped get the women to the retreat. Now, you can "pass the baton" to the other leaders. They will pick up where you left off in making this retreat a wonderful and memorable event!

Pray for the other leaders and the ladies attending. Pray that this retreat will have a powerful impact on everyone involved!

Thank you for serving "as His Feet,"
Cheris, the retreat writer

Food Leader and Decorations Leader

"Fancy Footwork-er"

(Responsibilities, retreat material, and checklist)

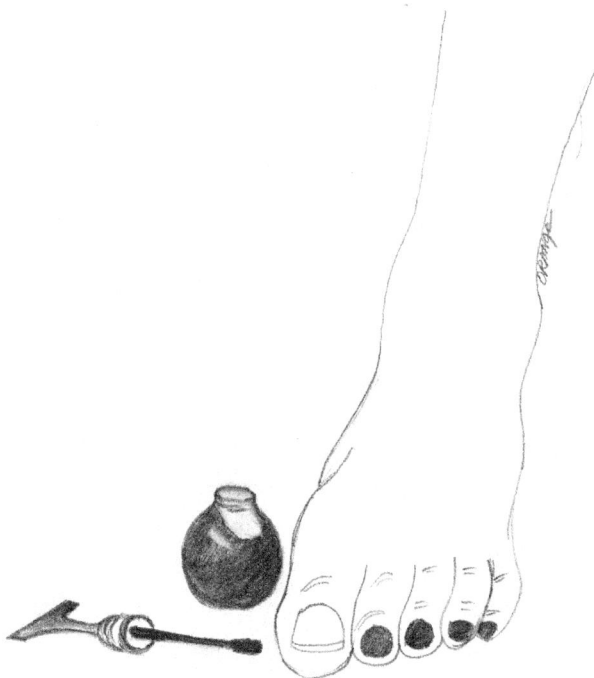

Food and decoration leader's responsibilities

If you were chosen to be the food and decoration leader, you are probably known for your talents in the kitchen or you have great organizational skills when it comes to taking care of details. You know how important food is to a successful retreat. Not only do you need to feed your hungry guests so they can concentrate on the retreat material, but they also need the sweet fellowship that takes place between friends during the meal and snack times. Eating and fellowship come together as a package deal at many church events. So, if you are willing to serve the other ladies by serving as the food leader, you will be a special blessing to them, and no one will go home hungry due to poor planning.

. . . .

Before the retreat

Pray

Before you begin, pray. Pray that God will lead you to make wise decisions in your planning.

Estimate how many guests

You and the chairperson need to estimate how many you think might attend the retreat. Be positive when thinking of a number since you're praying about this retreat. When you come up with a number, add a few more because God will work on the hearts of women as the promotional leader does her part. This number will help you plan. By the date of the registration deadline, you should know exactly how many are coming.

Considerations

Before you decide on a menu, think of several different options while also considering:

- how convenient the food is to make and time needed to prepare the food for people
- convenience of transportation of food and supplies needed
- if kitchen is available at the retreat setting, and if so, if it will accommodate your needs in preparation of the food
- the prices of various food items
- and time of year for the retreat.

All of these facts need to be considered before you commit to serving food at the retreat. If you decide to prepare the food yourself, don't pick your most complicated recipes! Keep it simple. Even though the food is a very nice part of the retreat, it is not the focal point.

The food should be served quickly with minimal cleaning up to do so that you and any volunteers helping you can enjoy the retreat as well. As a retreat leader, you need to participate in the retreat as much a possible.

Also, remember that if the church does not provide compensation for the cost of food that you have to prepare, you need to work the cost of food into your registration price. Talk to your chairperson about this before a registration price is set. Since you need to have the money to buy the food and supplies, it's probably best to wait until after the registration deadline to do any purchasing. (Make sure you keep all of your receipts from your purchasing).

Dinner options

You are in charge of planning dinner. The final menu is up to you as leader. You know what you can handle with the number of people you know will be attending. However, if you would like some suggestions, I am going to give you several options that stress convenience, quick preparation/ clean-up, and low costs:

1. Make dinner a "potluck" dinner. This option is the easiest on you. If you decide on this option, you can place flyers on the registration table for participants to pick up as they register. The flyers would need to explain that the dinner is a "potluck" dinner and list any instructions you may have. On the flyer you could inform the guests that you will provide tea, bread, salad, and salad dressing. In this way, you would get plenty of meats, vegetables, fruit dishes, and desserts.

2. Have a carefully planned "Bring-a-dish" dinner. This is a modified version of the "potluck" dinner, except you can call participants and tell them what type of dish to bring; furthermore, you can have a sign-up list at the registration table where they list their names under a certain type of dish to bring. In this option, you know how many of which types of food are coming and can add something if you need to do so after looking at the sign-up list. If you're making calls, you're in more control of what's coming. You can still provide tea, bread, salad, and salad dressing.

3. At a spring/summer retreat, a "brown bag" dinner might work well. Just have participants bring a sandwich, chips and a cold drink. You could provide a dessert. Again, you

need to promote this kind of dinner by making a flyer to be handed out at registration.

4. At a fall/winter retreat, a chili supper might work well. You could have some volunteers bring a crock-pot of chili for about every eight guests. Some volunteers could bring twelve baked potatoes, while others could bring a sheath cake. Figure a sheath cake for about every twelve guests. You could provide tea, salad, salad dressing, butter, sour cream, salt, pepper, and cheese.

5. Have half of the participants bring a tray/plate of finger foods and the other half could bring desserts. Let guests know by making calls or putting a sign-up list on the registration table. If you choose this option, you could put some of the desserts out for dinner, and save the rest for the late evening fellowship. You could provide tea for dinner.

6. Do whatever works best for you and your church ladies. Your church may provide a catered meal for events like this one. Just remember this is a fun, casual retreat. You aren't necessarily looking for a fancy or expensive dinner.

Fellowship desserts

The next time there's a need for food is the fellowship time after each guest has finished praying with her prayer partner. This is the last event before retiring for some sleep. Again, you could choose from several options. Just remember that if you choose options that require people to bring items, share the load equally among the participants. Example: If one person is bringing a pot of chili for dinner, then, you need someone else to bring a dessert for the fellowship time. Listed below are some fellowship dessert options:

1. If you choose option #5 on the dinner options, your desserts are already taken care of for the night.

2. Several volunteers could bring a plate of brownies, cookies, or some other kind of sweet snack.

3. Several volunteers could bring one of the following: a large bowl of chips, bowl of dip, vegetable tray, or large bowl of pretzels.

4. Several volunteers could bring one of the items in #2, while others could bring an item from #3 to make a combination of sweet and salty snacks.

5. If you have an idea of your own that you like, go with it.

Since the fellowship is soon after the session emphasizing Mary Magdalene's service to the Lord, put a large bowl of M&M's near the other desserts. Then, tape a sign in front of the bowl that says, "What kind of candy should make you think of service? M&M's (Mary Magdalene)"

The candy will add a little fun to the fellowship. (The chairperson will be handing out M&M's to the winners of a service-oriented game. If you provide candy at the fellowship, then everyone gets to enjoy them!). Besides, maybe from then on, whenever the guests see an M&M, they will be reminded of the retreat and Mary Magdalene's heart for service.

You also need to provide cold drinks. The amount of ice, ice chests, and cold drinks you need to bring depends on the number of people coming. If you have a large group, you get some help from volunteers. (Don't forget to ice the drinks down in ice-filled ice chests. You may also want to provide decaffeinated coffee. Don't forget to plug in the coffeemakers and put out sugar, sugar substitute, creamer, and spoons).

Breakfast

Your last food responsibility will be breakfast on Saturday morning. For breakfast, you might want to lean toward having a breakfast buffet. You could serve muffins, bagels, and fresh fruit.

Bring ice chests filled with individual containers of milk and orange juice. The amount of ice chests and breakfast drinks depends on the number of guests you have attending. You may need to ask volunteers to help you with this if you have a large group attending.

If you can, provide coffee again, and don't forget the condiments mentioned in the last section.

. . . .

Whichever options you choose for all three eating occasions, sit down and make a list of all food items that will be served at the retreat and how much will be needed. Then, if you have any calls to make in order to find volunteers to bring food, you can record who's bringing what and the exact amount she needs to bring in order to meet your food needs.

After choosing your option for each occasion, here's a space to write what you need. Write a "Y" by those things you need to provide and a person's name by what she is bringing.

Dinner items needed:

Fellowship dessert items needed:

Breakfast items needed:

Don't forget to make a list of all the things you may need to take to the retreat setting in order to serve everyone and to clean it up adequately. You may need to see the retreat place or call someone who knows about it to see what items may or may not be provided.

Some non-food items you may need to put on your list are: plates, pots/teapots to boil tea, pitchers for tea, Styrofoam cups, paper or plastic cups, napkins, trash bags, eating utensils, tablecloths, dish cloths, dish towels, dishwashing liquid, pot holders, paper towels, ice, ice chests, salad bowls, aluminum foil, plastic wrap, and coffee maker(s).

Here's a space to record what you need to take to the retreat that are not food items:

Time to eat

At the retreat

Note: Be prepared to serve the ladies before they get there.

Check your itinerary and be ready at the following times:

- After the welcome/prayer the ladies will be heading your way for "Sole" food (dinner).
- After the prayer partners have finished praying together, they will be coming your way for "Footloose" (fellowship desserts).
- On Saturday morning, the ladies will be coming to eat or "Fuel the feet" (breakfast).

Decoration leader's responsibilities

Not only have you been chosen as the food leader, you have also been selected to be the decorations leader. You will add some "extras" to the retreat that will help bind the theme-related material to the setting. The speaker will have some decorations/props in her area, the promotional leader will be responsible for the props in her skits, and the music leader will have made a few keepsakes for the guests, so you only need to make a few more visuals to complement everything else that has already been worked into other leaders' responsibilities.

Be sure that the registration price compensates you for the supplies that you need. Talk to the chairperson before the registration price is set. See if the church can pay for the supplies until you receive the money from the registration fees. Keep your receipts from your purchases.

You will only be asked to make three types of decorations. Two of them will be located in the meal/food area. The three decoration ideas and instructions are listed below.

Decorations

1. Make theme-related tablecloths. Buy white paper tablecloths, blue paint, and a sponge. Cut the sponge into the shape of a footprint. Dip the "footprint" into the paint and dab many "footprints" in all different directions on the tablecloths. Let the tablecloths dry, then put the tablecloths on the tables, and tape the tablecloths to the tables at the corners. Try to keep the tape from showing by folding the tablecloth and taping underneath the tables. You can place the tablecloths on the dinner tables and/or the serving tables.

2. Put a brand new pair of "closed-back" slippers on each

dinner table to serve as the centerpieces. Slip some fresh flowers or cascading green ivy into the foot-hole of each slipper for a soft, pretty look.

3. Tape at least three sets of footprints made out of white or black poster board onto the floor at each entrance or doorway to all of the rooms you will be using at the retreat setting. Place the "Footprints" in a sequence as if showing where someone has walked. This decoration will tie every used room to the retreat. You don't want the ladies to go to far without being reminded of feet/shoes and the significance of what they represent in relationship to Christ and His feet.

Food and decoration leader's checklist:

Before the retreat

- ❑ Pray for guidance in making decisions pertaining to the retreat.
- ❑ Estimate early with the chairperson on how many will attend the retreat. (Aim high).
- ❑ Read the "considerations" in your section of this book before proceeding to make decisions about what food to eat at the retreat.
- ❑ In planning, keep things as simple as possible.
- ❑ Talk to the chairperson about being compensated for food purchases in the registration price; that is, if you are buying anything.
- ❑ Look at suggested food options.
- ❑ Pick from these options or come up with your own ideas while emphasizing simplicity in preparation, transportation, serving, cleaning up, and expenses.
- ❑ Make a list of all food items you will need.
- ❑ If choosing to ask volunteers to bring needed items, call them and record what they will bring.
- ❑ Make a list of all non-food items you will need.
- ❑ Get the money you need for the purchases you will buy from the registration fees soon after the registration deadline has passed.
- ❑ Buy all food and non-food items you are responsible for bringing.
- ❑ Talk to the chairperson about money for the supplies for decorations.
- ❑ Buy the needed supplies for the tablecloths, the "slipper" centerpieces, and the poster board "footprints."
- ❑ Make theme-related tablecloths.

❑ Make "slipper" centerpieces.

❑ Make _____ sets of poster board "footprints. "(You will need to know how many door entrances there are at the retreat setting).

Day of the retreat

❑ Prepare and pack any food you are responsible for bringing.

❑ Take all of your needed food and non-food items to the retreat setting, including decorations.

❑ Put all of your decorations in place.

❑ Help other ladies with early set-up at the retreat setting if you're not still in the process of getting food prepared at the retreat setting.

❑ Retreat ready! Come to the retreat wearing slippers.

❑ Be at the retreat setting early at the chairperson's designated time.

At the retreat

❑ Serve with a smile at each of the three food occasions!

❑ Clean up after each food occasion with contentment in your heart, knowing that you just served Him well.

After the retreat

❑ Take care of the kitchen, "leftovers", and the belongings you brought, including your decorations.

❑ Go home, and rest.

❑ Write hand-written thank you notes to any volunteers who helped you at the retreat.

Dear Food/Decorations leader,

Thank you so much for your willingness to serve in more than one capacity. The Lord helped you persevere, and now you can look back at all you did and view your work as rewarding accomplishments for Him. Now that you know what He can do through you, maybe next time it will be easier to "step" forward when He asks you to do something for Him again.

Thank you for serving "as His feet,"
Cheris, the retreat writer

Music Leader and "Keepsake" Maker

"Toe-Tapper"

(Responsibilities, retreat material, and checklist)

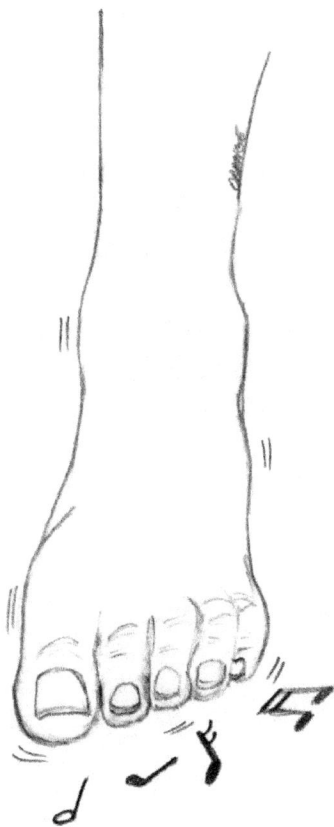

Music leader responsibilities

If you were selected to be the music leader, you probably have been blessed with musical talents or you're sensitive to what souls may need in the area of music to be rejuvenated and feel refreshed. As the music leader, you will be leading the group to worship our Lord and leading each person to reflect on her spiritual relationship to God. Your work will be very important as the music will soothe and reinforce what will be discussed at the retreat.

Pray

Begin your responsibilities by praying. Pray that the Lord will prepare your heart and enable you to make wise decisions as you go through the process of selecting music and deciding the best ways to lead/share music in your designated times at the retreat.

There may be times when God may lead you in singing praise choruses, or He may lead you to do something more dramatic to touch hearts more powerfully. Use His wisdom in making decisions that will affect the impact you will make on the ladies of your church.

As the writer of the retreat material, I will tell you what type of material will be preceding and following your designated times of music—this is to make sure that the content of the music can be "in tune" with what is being said around your time allotments. I may even give you suggestions that you can consider in your planning. But if you have a musical background with a large musical collection from which to select, I advise that you and the Holy Spirit make the final decisions. With prayer and His guidance, you will not be steered wrongly.

Pray for His power, plan with His wisdom, prepare and practice with diligence, and don't forget to have fun and be enriched yourself. Many times as leaders, we can be blessed in our own journey to enrich others.

Consider retreat setting/Chairperson

You will also have to consider your retreat setting in making your retreat plans. If you're in a home for the retreat, you will not need to have sound equipment and microphones ready, but you will in a church sanctuary because of its larger size.

You may want to come up with several ideas for each music time and then talk with the chairperson about your ideas before making your final decisions about what will work best in the program. You may also want to talk to the chairperson about sound equipment because this is something she also needs to consider in reference to meeting the needs of the other leaders, as well.

. . . .

Your responsibilities at the retreat

Background Music

The first time for music may not be designated on the itinerary sheet. Take advantage of times when no structured speaking is taking place. It would be a very nice touch to have music playing on a stereo/ sound system at the beginning of the retreat when guests are arriving and when they are eating dinner. This would be a great way to set the mood for the retreat. You could play tapes/CD's that give a relaxed, soothing feeling. My suggestion would be the inspirational music of Twila Paris, a contemporary Christian artist. If you select another singer, just remember that the first study session will be emphasizing resting in the Lord. Always remember to stop the music whenever a leader stands to speak.

Other good times to play background music that are not listed on the itinerary would be at the last fellowship time that evening and during breakfast on the next morning.

Foot Soak

The first structured time of music on the itinerary is called, "Foot Soak" and is described in the participant's books as refreshing music. The chairperson, "Big Toe," will have just given an overview of where the material is headed in the retreat. Following your time of music there will be the first session from the retreat speaker entitled, "At His Feet." In her session, she will be speaking about how we need to come to the Father daily to be refreshed: resting in Him, praising Him, studying His Word, and building a strong relationship with Him through prayer so that the way we live our lives can be totally affected by the impact He has had on us. The Bible character emphasis will be on Mary, the sister of Martha.

You will have about 10 minutes in this segment. Leading them in several praise choruses would be appropriate and refreshing. You might want to choose slower, reflective type music. It would be nice if you or someone else attending the retreat could play a guitar during this session. Guitars can have a way of reminding people of other times they "got away from it all" such as when they sat around a campfire singing songs when they were younger. If someone would like to sing a solo, the song, "At His Feet" sung by Natalie Grant, is a very nice song for this segment.

"Toe-Tappin' Time"

The next time you sing with the group it will be "Toe-tappin' time," which will be right after break time. This will be before the speaker's second study session entitled, "As His Feet", which will concentrate on service and the Bible character, Mary Magdalene. This session is after a break and is about service or "doing," so I think some upbeat music would be appropriate. You can lead faster praise music that encourages clapping with the beat or perhaps you have something creative in mind that encourages women to serve the Lord.

Again, you have about 10 minutes. Whatever you pick, have a good praise time and have fun!

"In Honor of His Feet"

The next designated music time on the itinerary is Saturday morning. The music session is entitled, "In Honor of His Feet," and is described in the participants' books as "more than music." This session will follow "Foot stretch" where the chairperson will lead the group through some in-place exercises. This will make them think of their dependence on God. The rest of the retreat following this music time will be emphasizing complete faith in God while remembering the important role of Jesus' feet throughout His ministry on earth that led to Him being nailed to the cross.

I described this musical occasion as "more than music" because I want you to add another dimension to this particular time. Think of ladies in your church that might have a gift or an ability that they can share along with music. For example, you or someone could sing a solo while another person beautifully "signs" the words with sign language. Maybe someone could use chalk to sketch and create an awe-inspiring picture while a song is being played on an instrument. The idea is to stimulate the group's sense of sight as well as sound. The group will walk away with a visual memory—not just the memory of pretty music. Also, it shows the women how God can use other abilities to glorify Him in worship when we're receptive to being used.

If you want a beautiful song to be sung or played while also allowing someone to "do" something while the music is being sung or played, pick music that would be appropriate. If we all would be willing to be vessels used by Him, there is no limit to what He may convict us to do in order to truly touch the lives of others. For His sake, try something new. It may require searching to discover the abilities of the women in your church, more practice, or more difficulty in reaching the desired result. But it will be worth the effort as you skillfully put together a combination of gifts for the cause of Christ! A beautiful song that could be played on a tape/CD is the song by the Christian artist, Steve Green, entitled, "Find Us Faithful." This song is very moving and speaks of "the footprints that we leave." If you don't use this song in this segment, you may want to use it in the next responsibility you have.

The speaker's final study session, "Because of the Master's Feet," will deal with Christ's life of service and the sacrificial gift of His life. The women will be challenged to do whatever the Lord places on their hearts that morning.

"A Time for Him"

The last time there is a need for music is toward the end of the retreat. After the speaker's last session, "Because of the Master's Feet," she will encourage the group to respond to whatever the Lord has placed on their hearts that morning by coming to the foot of the cross and praying. She will have a cross leaning against a wall behind her. At this time, the women will be making a commitment to have a time for Him "at His feet" and "as His feet" if they choose to do so. Since this is a reflective time for participants, playing some quiet, soft Christian music from the stereo/ sound system would be nice as they think about what they want to do. Continue the music throughout this entire time, as some may come to the front to pray; however, stop the music before guests share testimonies or prayer requests with the group.

. . . .

*Not only have you been selected as music leader, but you have also received the responsibility of being the "keepsake" maker.

. . . .

Responsibilities of "keepsake" maker

If you're artistically inclined in the area of music, I'm hoping you also like the adventure of craft making. You and any volunteers you enlist will need to make a bookmark and nametag for each participant attending the retreat. You may begin making these items any time after you purchase the materials needed to make them.

Registration Price

Talk to your chairperson about the amount of money needed to make the purchases. Your expenses should be considered when the registration price is being considered. See if the church will pay for the expenses until the money is received from the registration money. As a leader, you don't need to have to pay for expenses in order to carry out your responsibilities.

Volunteers

As mentioned before, you may use the help of volunteers. You could schedule a "get-together" with your volunteers and have a day of crafts and fellowship. But don't reveal the subject material or events at the retreat to your volunteers. Keep everyone curious. This keeps the excitement level high!

You and your volunteers will have fun making these crafts. As leader though, it is your responsibility to make sure the crafts are assembled well, complete before the retreat, and given to the promotional leader when needed.

Bookmark

One craft you will need to make is the "Feet of Faith" bookmark. The participants can place their bookmarks in their Bibles to serve as a reminder of what they learned in the "Feet of Faith" exercise and during the share time following it. You and your volunteers can pass out the bookmarks after the discussion that follows the "Feet of Faith" exercise.

The supplies needed for the bookmarks are: a white poster board and a black poster board for about every fifty attending, glue, a bandana for about every twelve people attending, a white paint pen, and a hole-puncher. Instructions and a diagram for the bookmark are provided below.

Instructions for the bookmarks:

*Make as many bookmarks as there are participants.

1. Make a pattern of the cross, and outline as many as you need on the white poster boards. Then, cut them out.

2. Cut the base of the bookmarks out of the black poster boards. Each bookmark should be 6"x 2".

3. Punch a hole with a hole-puncher near the top of the bookmark in the center.

4. Tie a slender 4" piece of the red bandana material in a knot through the hole.

5. Glue the 3½" cut red bandana material on the black poster board in the center of the bookmark.

6. Glue the white cross in the center of the red bandana.

7. At the top of the bookmark, below the hole, and above the bandana material, write:

    Feet of Faith: "…follow him…"

    (Use the white paint pen to do the writing).

8. Cut out two small footprints for each bookmark, and glue a set of footprints on each bookmark. Place the footprints as if they are walking to the foot of the cross.

9. At the bottom of the bookmark on the black poster board, write:

    John 10:4 (NIV).

Diagram of the bookmark:

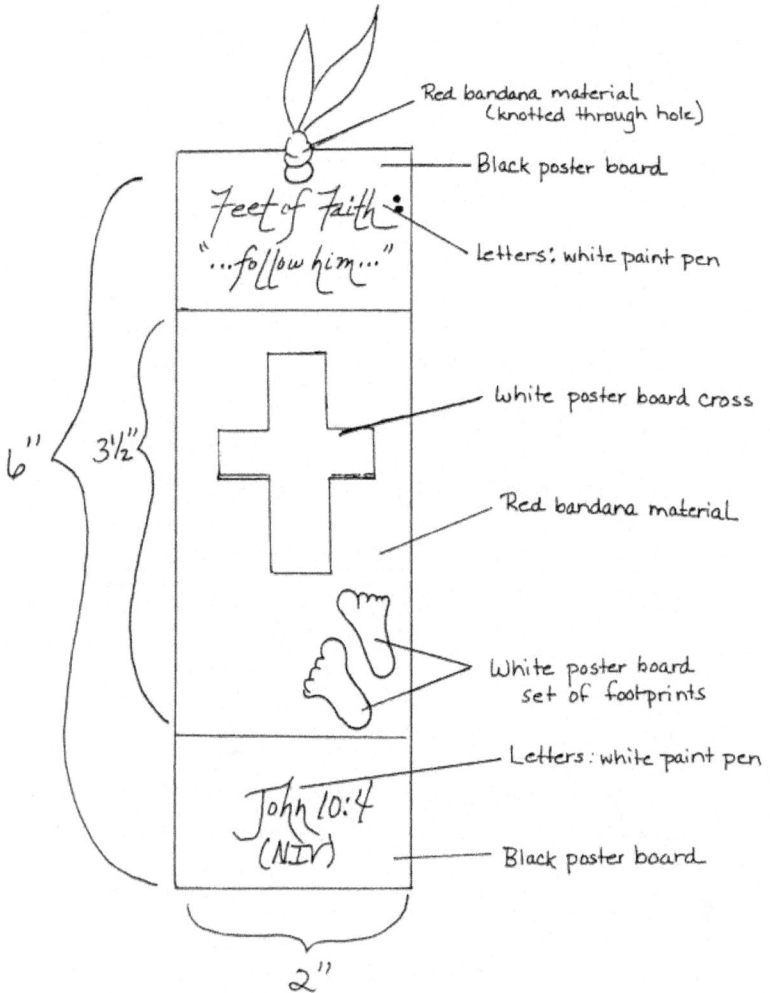

Red bandana material
(knotted through hole)

Black poster board

Feet of Faith:
"...follow him..."

Letters: white paint pen

White poster board cross

Red bandana material

White poster board
set of footprints

Letters: white paint pen

John 10:4
(NIV)

Black poster board

6"   3½"   2"

"Slipper" Nametags

The other craft needed is a "slipper" nametag for each participant. The nametag will actually look like a slipper. They will take a little extra work, but you will have fun making them and will be proud of the results. Since we want this retreat to be memorable, we need to start off in a creative way and not just hand the guests a press-on adhesive label!

The supplies needed for the "slipper" nametag are: material that looks like what a slipper is made out of (such as terry cloth or similar material), white poster board for about every fifty participants attending, glue, slender cloth ribbon, double-sided tape or clips, and narrow multi-purpose adhesive labels to go on the heel part of the "slipper." You can use old or cheap washcloths and get about four to six nametags out of each standard washcloth. Instructions and a diagram are provided below.

Instructions for the "slipper" nametags:

*Make as many slipper nametags as you have participants.

1. On a piece of paper, trace the bottom of the slipper shown on the diagram. Cut the new pattern out.

2. On a piece of paper, trace the top of the slipper on the diagram. Cut the new pattern out.

3. Outline the new pattern of the heel on the washcloth material and the white poster board. Cut both of them out.

4. Outline the new pattern of the top part of the slipper on the washcloth material. Cut it out.

5. Glue the material of the heel on the poster board heel.

6. Glue the material of the top piece on the material of the heel.

7. Stick an adhesive multi-purpose label on the material of the heel.

8. Add a bow made of cloth ribbon on the top piece of the slipper.

9. To be able to fasten the nametag to your shirt, you can buy double-sided tape and attach it to the back, or you can use clips which can clip to the "slipper" and a shirt.

Diagram of "slipper" nametag:

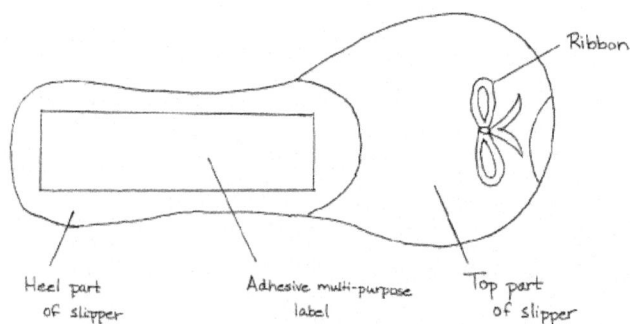

Heel part of slipper   Adhesive multi-purpose label   Top part of slipper   Ribbon

Music leader and "keepsake" maker's checklist:

Before the retreat

- ❏ Pray.
- ❏ Consider retreat setting and decide if you need sound equipment or any particular instruments brought with you.
- ❏ Select and find music that would be appropriate at each designated music time or at other times.
- ❏ Talk with the chairperson about your music ideas and the possible need for sound equipment.
- ❏ Find out if any women have gifts that could be combined with music during your "In Honor of His Feet" segment.
- ❏ Contact any women who will be helping you with the worship music, and schedule practice times.
- ❏ Rehearse with those who are helping you.
- ❏ Select tapes/CDs for the retreat welcome, dinner, fellowship, breakfast, and the end of the final study session.
- ❏ Talk to the chairperson about getting money for your supplies to make the "keepsakes. "
- ❏ Buy supplies for bookmarks and nametags.
- ❏ Find volunteers to help make retreat "keepsakes", and tell them the scheduled date to get together to make "keepsakes".
- ❏ Make the "keepsakes".
- ❏ Get the nametags to the promotional leader.

Day of the retreat

❑ Help with set-up at the retreat place early in the day, if possible.

❑ Pack music, instruments, stereo, bookmarks, equipment (if needed) and whatever else to make the music sessions run smoothly.

❑ Retreat ready! Arrive early, and come wearing slippers.

❑ Lead the three music sessions as planned. Have any instruments and/or equipment ready to use when needed.

❑ Play background music for the guests' arrival, dinner, scheduled fellowship, breakfast, and "Time for Him."

❑ Hand out bookmarks after the discussion on the "Feet of Faith" worksheet.

After the retreat

❑ Help clean up the retreat setting.

❑ Go home, and rest!

❑ Write hand-written thank-you notes to anyone who helped you before and during the retreat to fulfill your responsibilities.

Dear Music leader/"Keepsake" maker,

Thank you so much for being willing to serve. You will touch the hearts of many through songs. Also, you will send home little special reminders of a wonderful weekend spent resting "at the feet of Jesus." Part of leading well is serving well. Pray that God will strengthen you in both areas to accomplish His goals for your life.

> Thank you for serving "as His feet,"
> Cheris, retreat writer

Speaker/Study Session Leader

"Foot Specialist"
(Responsibilities, retreat material, and checklist)

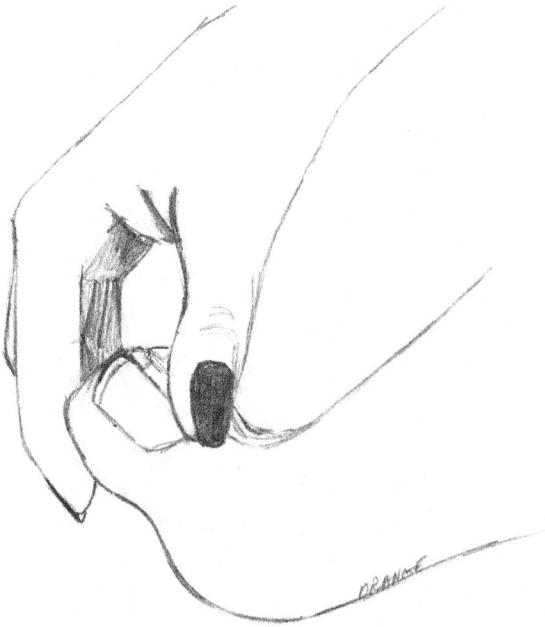

Speaker/Study session leader-responsibilities

If you were selected to be the speaker/study session leader, you are probably known as the one who enjoys spending time in God's Word. Hopefully, you're not afraid to stand in front of a group to speak. If you are nervous about the idea of speaking in public, think about these things: God will stand with you, and the importance of sharing from His Word far outweighs the need to sit and be comfortable. In fact, parts of this retreat deal with the issue of "getting out of your comfort zone" in order to serve the Lord. God will prepare your heart and mind in the weeks leading up to the retreat. He only asks that you be willing to serve as speaker/study session leader, and let Him work through you. The notes provided will serve you well as you prepare to teach.

. . . .

Before the retreat
(How to prepare)

Prayer

Pray. Ask God to prepare you for this teaching assignment. If there are issues or problems you've been dealing with, lay them at the feet of Jesus. Let Him take care of the difficult situations in your life, and you concentrate on serving Him well.

Read and Study

Read over all of the material in your section. Take notes as you read, and become very comfortable and familiar with the Bible passages, verses, and instructional speaking parts.

Study Session Worksheets

First, you will be provided with the worksheets that the participants have in their books. Then, you will be guided through the worksheet and given instructions as to what you should say on each part of the worksheet. Because of the structured format of the worksheets, most of your time will be spent reading the material and practicing the delivery of it, rather than researching. Feel free to research and learn as much as you would like about the scriptures before the retreat. Writing on note cards or directly on your worksheet might be beneficial to you in reference to practicing the delivery of your material.

Delivery

When you go in front of the ladies to speak, hopefully, you'll have a stand where you can place your materials. You may carry your Bible, leader book with worksheets, and speaking notes, any needed props, and note cards you made for presenting the delivery, if you choose to do so.

Be so comfortable and familiar with the material that when you stand to speak, you are conversational in your style. Don't simply read the material or memorize it. (But you need to read the scripture so that it will not be misquoted).

As you practice, remember to look up at the audience so that you will be able to make eye contact, as much as possible, with the ladies in the group. If you would like, you can practice in front of a mirror.

Since the participants will get as much out of the sessions as you put into them, give 100%. As it says in Colossians 3: 23, "Whatever you do, work at it with all your heart, as working for the Lord, not for men" (NIV). Start with enthusiasm, continue with enthusiasm, and end with enthusiasm! You are there to motivate people into action. So encourage, inspire, and let the life you live be an example of what you're talking about in the study sessions. You are part of the delivery!

Props/Displays

If any props or displays will be needed to make a stronger impact on the audience, you will be provided with that information before the notes of each study session. Visuals can help an audience remember what they have heard. Besides, using creativity and imagination is a wonderful way to capture and retain the audience's attention!

Just make sure you practice your delivery of the material while including the use of all props or displays. Practicing with them will keep you from forgetting to use them in your actual delivery at the retreat.

Volunteers

If you use any volunteers in your study sessions, be sure to contact them before the retreat and tell them exactly what their responsibilities are and what session(s) they will be needed. Notifying them beforehand will keep them from being surprised, and it will also give you one less responsibility at the retreat. Example: Call Pam, and ask her if she will read the scripture in Colossians 2:6–7 and say the opening prayer at the beginning of the "As His Feet" study session. If she says she will help you, tell her that this study session is the second session you lead, and she will see it listed in the itinerary in her retreat book. Tell her you will come forward to speak after she reads the scripture and prays.

· ·

At the retreat

*Check your itinerary. Your first study session will follow "Foot Soak" which is refreshing music led by the music leader and before the skit, "To Be or Not To Be."

"At His feet" worksheet for study session 1
Mary, the sister of Martha

Scriptures:
Luke 10:38–41;
John 11:19–35,43–44;
and John 12:1–8

When we spend time "at His feet," we will be like Mary:

"P"- _____

"E"- _____

"R"- _____

"F"- _____

"U"- _____

"M"- _____

"E"- _____

1. Worries become _____ and faith becomes
_____. Why? Because we lay our worries
"at His feet."

"Those who know your name will trust in you, for you, Lord,
have never forsaken those who seek you." (Psalm 9:10 NIV).
You: _____ God: _____

"You will keep in perfect peace him whose mind is steadfast, because he trusts in you." (Isaiah 26:3 NIV). You:
_____ God: _____

"He gives strength to the weary and increases the power of
the weak." (Isaiah 40:29 NIV). You: _____
God: _____

"When anxiety was great within me, your consolation brought joy to my soul." (Psalm 94:19 NIV). You: _____ _____ God: _____

2. Worship becomes _____. Why? Because we _____ our praises to Him.

   Psalms 7:17 says, "I will give thanks to the Lord because of his righteousness and will sing praise to the name of the Lord most high." (Psalm 7:17 NIV).

3. The Word lights the _____ . How?

   As we choose to _____ it, we will choose to _____.

   "Your word is a lamp to my feet and a light for my path." (Psalm 119:105 NIV).

   *As we read God's Word daily, we will strive to _____ _____ like Him and to _____ like Him.

"At His feet" teaching notes:

Props: Bc sure to come wearing slippers.

Special instructions: Be sure to read the scriptures aloud. Also, when the group is filling in information on their worksheets, give them time to do so before you continue speaking.

Introduction

Speaker: "When I come wearing slippers, I'm ready to rest 'at Jesus' feet'. Let's bow for prayer before we learn about the importance of being 'at His feet.'" (Prayer)

"When you rest in Him, you share, you praise, and you listen as He speaks to you. Let's turn in our Bibles to look at Mary, the sister of Martha. As we look at each of these scripture passages, be thinking of what Mary's heart is like and what we can learn from her. In the scripture references we will be looking at this evening, you will see Mary returning again and again to be at the Master's feet."

Study session

"Let's turn to Luke 10:38–41." (Pause for the group to respond, then, read the scripture aloud).

"Here we see Martha, Mary's sister, busy with preparations while Mary is spending time with Christ. Mary is 'at His feet' learning from Him and cherishing the time spent in His presence. Friends, this passage speaks straight to our hearts. Yes, we will be busy with the many things on our 'to do' lists. But no action is more important than resting at Jesus' feet to allow Him to fill us with His love, His wisdom, His comfort, and His guidance. In our own flesh, we will want to accomplish and get all things done so that no one will see us as lazy or unable to perform the tasks before us. We want to be seen as dependable. But why not come into His presence each day and depend on Him to give you what He desires you to have so that you can truly 'be' as His child? Yes, rest at His feet and desire a heart like His.

"Now, if you'll turn to our next passage of scripture found in John 11:19–35, then look at verses 43–44" (Pause for the group to respond and have a volunteer to read the scriptures aloud). "_____, please stand and read the scripture references for us." (The scriptures are read).

"This time when we see Mary, her heart is broken over the death of her brother,

Lazarus. In verse 29, it says, 'upon hearing Jesus was there, she got up quickly and went to him.' Verse 32 tells what Mary said to Jesus, 'Lord, if you had been here, my brother would not have died,' Her faith was strong in that she believed that if Christ had been there, Lazarus would not have died. In verse 33, it says, 'When Jesus saw her weeping…he was deeply moved in spirit and troubled.' He felt her pain as He feels yours today and always. Christ had a great love for Mary, but also for the Jews who had come with her, Martha, and Lazarus. Christ hurt for those He loved because He is our gentle Shepherd who loves deeply. Friends, doesn't this show you that when you hurt, Jesus hurts with you? In verse 35, it says, 'Jesus wept.' We should not be ashamed of tears. Christ wept, showing us a window into His own heart. Then we see He defied death by bringing Lazarus back to life as it says in verses 43 and 44. He is a God of miracles! Remember that the next time you want to give up hope in a situation before you.

"When Mary's heart was broken, she fell at His feet. When you are burdened, fall at Jesus' feet. Go to Him first and lovingly lay it all before Him. No one will understand your pain or your problems like Jesus will. He's lovingly waiting as you run toward Him. Never hesitate! Run and fall at His feet!

"The last reference we will look at involving Mary is John 12:1–8. Please turn there as we read again." Pause for guests to respond, then, read the scripture passage aloud. "The pouring of the perfume was a selfless act of love for Mary. She was so filled with gratitude and adoration that her attention was solely on Him. She had no need to explain her actions because the entire time her focus was on pleasing the Father, not others. Can you imagine the sweet aroma that filled the room that day? In spite of the value of the expensive perfume, Mary was the more valuable perfume 'at His feet'. Her sweet aroma was her loving heart for Jesus her Lord. When God looks at your heart in reference to Him, would He be able to characterize it as a sweet aroma in the condition it is today? If not, there are some things you need to face and settle in His presence today. You may need a fresh start.

"If we are willing to commit to be at the 'feet of Jesus' everyday, we too can be like a sweet perfume in the presence of God. Looking at Mary, how can we be the perfume that God longs to see 'at His feet?'" Have the group write the phrase after each letter, then, you elaborate in sharing the comments that follow each phrase.

"Let's look at your worksheet as we fill in this acrostic of 'perfume'. To be like Mary, we need to be:

1. "P"-(portraying powerful acts of love). Even though her acts were simple, they were powerful because they were in such contrast to the normal reaction of what others were doing around her. Her actions from the heart were pleasing to Christ. First, she sat 'at His feet' to listen to Him. Secondly, she shared her sorrow with Him because she

loved both Jesus and her brother. Then, she poured the perfume over Jesus' feet out of love and gratitude for all that He had done for her. You need to portray powerful acts of love.

2. "E"-(Eager to learn, and be attentive to Him). Mary was so eager. He, not the meal preparations, was most important to her. She wanted to learn all she could from Him. You need to be so eager.

3. "R"-(Respond quickly to Him). She was quick to drop to His feet. Will you respond to Him as quickly? Be ready to respond.

4. "F"- (Faithful). She truly believed in Him and was committed in her love for Him. You continue to find Mary at Jesus' feet. Are you this faithful? Be at His feet!

5. "U"-(Unconcerned about what others thought when she focused on God). She didn't care about what others thought when she poured perfume on His feet. She truly sought to honor Him in all that she did. Stop trying to please others, and please God by loving Him most.

6. "M"-(Mindful of His authority). In His presence, she sat or fell to His feet. She also told Jesus about Lazarus, knowing that He was capable of making a difference in whether or not Lazarus lived or died. She was very aware of His power and authority. Are you mindful of the authority of Christ? If not, be mindful of His mighty power.

7. "E"-(Example). As she was an example to us, can you be an example to others, your children, or your grandchildren by coming to sit "at the Lord's feet' daily? Be the example,

and allow others to see how resting at Jesus' feet can make such an incredible difference in your heart for Him. Pray that you can be an example in this way and that many will follow your example for generations to come.

"What do you think will happen when we spend time 'at the Lord's feet'?

1. Worries become (weightless) and faith becomes (stronger). Why?

    Because we (lay) our worries 'at His feet.'

    "The worries are no longer ours but are with Him. We have the faith to know that He will take care of us.

    "Look at the verses in this section following # 1. Read each of them, and put in the lines that follow each verse: the action(s) of you and the response(s) of the Lord." Give the group time to answer. Then, give the correct answers.

    "In Psalm 9:10, if you (know His name, trust Him, and seek Him), God (will never forsake you). In Isaiah 26:3, if you (are steadfast and trust God), He (will keep you in perfect peace). In Isaiah 40:29, if you (are weary and weak), God (will give you strength and increase your power). In Psalm 94:19, if you (have great anxiety), God and His consolation (will bring you joy)."

2. Worship becomes (automatic). Why?

    Because we (lift) our praises to Him for all that He has done and all that He is.

"Worship is a natural response when you love Him greatly. Realize who He is, and praise him!

Psalm 7:17 says, 'I will give thanks to the Lord because of his righteousness and will sing praise to the name of the Lord most high.'"

3. The Word lights the (path). How?

As we choose to (learn) it, we will choose to (live) it!

"God has given us a precious guidebook to help us live our lives. It has to be more than a display on our coffee table. We must read it, learn it, and live it!

Psalm 119:105 says, 'Your word is a lamp to my feet and a light for my path.' (NIV)

"Amen and Amen again!
     *As we read God's Word daily, we will strive to (be) like Him and to (act) like Him."

"You must *be* before doing if you want the doing to be God-centered. The focus must be on Him and not on you. Remember, Mary had a beautiful heart. She wasn't looking in a mirror, but at the loving face of Jesus!"

Closing

(Motion both hands downward.) "Let us lay our worries 'at His feet." (Motion both hands upward.). "Let us lift up our praises to Him." (Open hands to imitate opening a book.) "And let us learn from His Word so that we will have a closer relationship to Him." (Put hands down.) "That is only the beginning of all that He has planned for us."

'For I know the plans I have for you' declares the Lord,

'plans to prosper you and not to harm you, plans to give you hope and a future.' (Jeremiah 29:11 NIV).

(Looking down) "Slippers, you were first." (Looking at the audience) "So, that means the next pair of shoes will be…" (Pause) "Oh, I can't tell you that. It would ruin the suspense for my next study session. So, until then, just sit back and relax. We can't move on just yet, because there's still someone in the building dealing with the issue of whether or not to come wearing slippers."

"Remember, it's important to be 'at His feet' before we do His work!" (Go back to your seat.)

· ·

*Check your itinerary. Your second study session will follow "Toe-tappin' time" and will be before the game, "Get Ready, Get Set, and Serve."

"As His Feet" (Today) worksheet
for study session 2
Mary Magdalene

Scriptures: Luke 8:1–3;
Mark 15:40–41; Matthew 27:61;
and Matthew 28:1–10

Look at Luke 8:1–3 for the answers:
    Mary Magdalene was formerly _____ and
    helped _____ Jesus' ministry.

Look at Mark 15:40–41 for the answers:
    Mary Magdalene was near the _____ at
    Jesus' _____.

    In Galilee, she cared for _____.

Look at Matthew 27:61 for the answer:
    Mary Magdalene was at the _____.

Look at Matthew 28:1–10 for the answers:
    Who did Mary Magdalene see? _____.

    How did she feel? _____.

    To whom did she go tell the good news?
    _____.

    How did she go? _____.

Servants should think on these things when they respond to
God's calling, and serve "as His feet:"

1.   "F"- _____ when you serve Him.

"Let us fix our eyes on Jesus, the author and perfecter of our faith…" (Hebrews 12:2 NIV).

*Mary Magdalene did not focus on her past, but she focused on God. She became a new creation with Christ.

"Therefore, if anyone is in Christ, he is a new creation the old has gone, the new has come!" (2 Corinthians 5:17 NIV).

2. "E"-_____, serve Him.

"For I am the Lord, your God, who takes hold of your right hand and says to you, 'Do not fear, I will help you.'" (Isaiah 41:13 NIV).

*Discipline yourself to respond to the Spirit. Follow Him and not the crowd.

3. "E"-_____ when you serve Him.

The "possible" refers to _____.

"Never be lacking in zeal, but keep your spiritual fervor, serving the Lord. Be joyful in hope, patient in affliction, faithful in prayer." (Romans 12:11–12 NIV).

*We will grow stronger through Christ as we depend less on ourselves and depend more on Him. Difficulties make us feel weak, but they turn us to God for strength.

"That is why, for Christ's sake, I delight in weaknesses, in insults, in hardships, in persecutions, in difficulties. For when I am weak, then I am strong." (2 Corinthians 12:10 NIV).

The "impossible" refers to _____.

- Look for changes in others.
- When God's involved, anything can happen!

4. "T"–_____ serve Him.

   "For the eyes of the Lord range throughout the earth to strengthen those whose hearts are fully committed to him…" (2 Chronicles 16:9 NIV).

"Submit yourselves then, to God. Resist the devil, and he will flee from you." (James 4:7 NIV).

"As His Feet" (Today) teaching notes:

Props: Flip-flops, a beach towel, a large jar of sand, a lawn chair, and tennis shoes

Set-up: Place the lawn chair center stage with the tennis shoes behind the chair. Place the jar of sand beside the chair. After a volunteer reads Colossians 2:6–7 and opens the session in prayer, the speaker comes forward wearing flip-flops and has a beach towel wrapped around her shoulders.

Special instructions: Be sure to read the scripture where it is noted in the notes to support what is being said. Also, when giving answers to the fill-in-the-blanks, give enough time for the participants to fill in their answers before continuing to speak.

Introduction

Volunteer: "So then, just as you received Christ Jesus as Lord, continue to live in him, rooted and built up in him, strengthened in the faith as you were taught, and overflowing with thankfulness." (Colossians 2:6–7 NIV). (She then leads the group in an opening prayer for this session).

Speaker: "I was wearing slippers, but while I was resting at the Lord's feet, I had such an attitude of gratitude, I had to come wearing flip-flops. You've got to be happy and thankful when you're walking on the beach, so these are the shoes that represent me walking with a thankful heart. Flip-flops come between slippers and…well, you'll see in a moment.

"You know how it is when you go on a vacation, and you're strolling along the beach. You look out over the water, and you see a beautiful setting sun." (Sigh.) "What a wonderful picture God has painted for you and everyone else around you who chooses to stop and be in awe of it!" (Pause.) "That's it!

The awe you feel looking at God's artistic sunset is much like the overflowing gratitude you feel toward God when you've continually been resting in Him. I know the sunset pales in comparison to God, but I'm trying to get you to capture the magnitude of fantastic feelings you can experience with God when He's at the center of your world. When you come to the place where you have a thankful heart for all God's done for you, you can't help but serve Him. Service is a natural outward expression of love and gratitude for God. With the blessings that come our way, we are to choose to be a blessing to others." (Put the towel on the ground in front of you and pick up the jar of sand.)

"See this jar of sand?" (Pour the sand onto the towel.) "If you can think of one family member or friend that you dearly love, that one person alone represents only one grain of sand. You can't list all of the blessings God has placed in your life. He has blessed you in more ways than there are grains of sand on this towel you see before you.

"Yet, just thinking of one very special blessing is enough to say, 'Thank you, God, I will serve you with total commitment as you have always shown great love for me!' With blessings, comes responsibility." (Put the jar down, step out of the flip-flops, get tennis shoes from behind the chair, sit in the chair, put the tennis shoes on your feet, and tie them.)

"I'm putting my tennis shoes on because I have some serving to do. (Stand up.) Let's look at a woman of God who served Him well."

Study session

"Turn in your Bible to Luke 8:1–3. (Read the scripture aloud.) We know from this passage that Mary Magdalene was formerly (possessed by demons) and helped (support) Jesus' ministry.

"Now, let's look at Mark 15:40–41. (Read aloud.) We know that Mary Magdalene was near the (cross) at Jesus' (crucifixion). In Galilee, she cared for (His needs).

"Let's look at Matthew 27:61. (Read aloud.) From this passage, we know that she was at the (burial). Now, turn to Matthew 28:1–10, and answer the questions on your worksheet." (Give the group a few minutes to answer then, go over the answers quickly.)

- Who did Mary Magdalene see? (She saw an angel.)
- How did she feel? (She was afraid yet filled with joy.)
- Who did she go tell the good news to? (She went to tell the disciples.)
- How did she go? (She was running.)

"While the sight of an angel frightened Mary Magdalene, we are often afraid of just serving the Lord. When the angel told Mary Magdalene to tell the good news, she ran quickly with joy in her heart. Like her, you may be afraid at first, but do you do what He says to do quickly and with joy? We all should, if we don't. Next time respond as Mary Magdalene did. Be quick to obey with joy in your heart!"

"Today, servants of God should do these four things to serve God well 'as His feet.' See if you do these things as we go through each one on this acrostic of 'feet.'" (Have the group write the phrase after each letter, then, you elaborate in sharing the comments that follow each phrase.)

1. "F"- (Focus on Him) when you serve Him.

'Let us fix our eyes on Jesus, the author and perfecter of our faith...' (Hebrews 12:2 NIV).

"If you focus on Him, you will be able to serve others with His help. If He is leading you through the task, He can take an ordinary person and make extraordinary things happen. If you have faith in Him, Christ's assurance will flood out the doubts and the 'I'm-not-good-enough's.' If you're thinking about what you're not, then you're not focusing on God."

"God only needs you to have a willing heart. He will do the rest. As Christians, we are the hands and feet that can do God's work for Him as we are used by Him and under His direction."

"Whatever 'past baggage' you may carry with you, you can lay them at the feet of Jesus. Think of Mary Magdalene. Because she had an attitude of gratitude toward Jesus, she served Him by supporting His ministry. She was formerly possessed by demons, but she didn't let her past keep her from serving others. She became a new creation in Christ."

'Therefore, if anyone is in Christ, he is a new creation; the old has gone, the new has come!' (2 Corinthians 5:17 NIV)

2. "E"- (Even if no one else goes), serve Him. If God has spoken to you about a way to serve Him, you must go, and be obedient. He has called you to 'step out in faith.' Your actions don't depend on the actions of others, but on your relationship to Jesus Christ. Don't fear going alone when the Lord goes with you.

'For I am the Lord, your God, who takes hold of your right hand and says to you, "Do not fear; I will help you." (Isaiah 41:13 NIV).

*Discipline yourself to respond to the Spirit. Follow Him and not the crowd.

3. "E"- (Expect the possible and/or the impossible) when you serve Him.

"The possible refers to (problems):

"Problems may happen, but God has allowed them for whatever reason. Either the problems will stretch you into being a better servant for God, or the problems will redirect you into having an even better result for the Lord. Remember that His plans are better than your own, even when you may not understand them at the time. Just keep 'stepping' as the Lord leads while having faith in His master plan. And most of all, pray through it all!"

"Don't be surprised if right before you're about to serve the Lord in an incredible way, your children get the chicken pox, you have a flat tire, your washing machine breaks, and you step in a hole and twist your ankle while taking out the trash. Life is unpredictable, stressful, and usually has a bad sense of timing. Keep praying, and God will get you through those difficult times."

'Never be lacking in zeal, but keep your spiritual fervor, serving the Lord. Be joyful in hope, patient in affliction, faithful in prayer.' (Romans 12:11–12 NIV).

*We will grow stronger through Christ as we depend less

on ourselves and depend more on Him. Difficulties make us feel weak, but they turn us to God for strength.

'That is why, for Christ's sake, I delight in weaknesses, in insults, in hardships, in persecutions, in difficulties. For when I am weak, then I am strong.' (2 Corinthians 12:10 NIV).

"The impossible refers to (miracles):

"As a result of the service you did for the Lord, you may see miracles such as, changes in the hearts of people where you thought changes were impossible. Allow God to work His master plan through you to impact the lives of others. Servants of God can also literally see a miracle with their own eyes. Mary Magdalene witnessed a miracle when she saw an angel after Jesus had been resurrected. She was also one of the first to believe the miracle that Jesus had risen from the dead. These events are recorded in Matthew 28:2–6."

4. "T"- (Through total commitment), serve Him.

"After Jesus' crucifixion, Mary Magdalene and others were so committed in their love for Him that they had gone back to the tomb after His death. Look at Matthew 28:8 again. After the angel told them Christ had risen, what was the response of the women, including Mary Magdalene?" (Listen as someone responds. Answer: They hurried, afraid yet filled with joy and ran to tell the disciples.) "They did not let their fear keep them from seeing the task be completed. Stay committed in your love for the Lord and by doing that, you stay committed to the task He gives you."

"For the eyes of the Lord range throughout the earth to strengthen those whose hearts are fully committed to him…" (2 Chronicles 16:9 NIV).

"He will help you see the task through to the end. When God reveals an area of service, decide from the beginning that you're totally committed to see the task through until the end, no matter what obstacles Satan puts in your way. Satan's ammunition to throw you off the track of service has to be confronted with the steadfast determination that God Himself would have against Satan."

"Submit yourselves, then, to God. Resist the devil, and he will flee from you." (James 4:7 NIV).

"Let your love for God be your motivation to keep you pressing on. Mary Magdalene showed her loving support until the end of Jesus' life by being at the cross and sharing in His sorrow. It had to be extremely difficult to see someone, you love hanging on a cross, pierced with nails. But in spite of the emotional pain it caused her to be there, she was there out of sincere love for Him. In serving the Lord, don't take the easy road. Take the road Jesus would take if He were in your place."

Closing:

"In doing service for the Lord, remember: focus on God, go even if no one but God goes with you, expect the possible and/or impossible, and remain totally committed to the Lord until His goals are achieved through you. (Look down at your shoes.)

"Tennis shoes, get ready to run the race.

'…let us run with perseverance the race marked out for us. Let us fix our eyes on Jesus, the author and perfecter of our faith, who for the joy set before him endured the cross, scorning its shame, and sat down at the right hand of the throne of God.' (Hebrews 12:1–2 NIV)."

(Get in running position as if to begin a race and say your next line loudly). "On your mark, get ready, get set, and…serve!" (Take off running to the back of the room as the chairperson comes up to give the directions for the game on service.)

. . . .

*Check your itinerary. Your third study session will be after the "Feet of Faith" worksheet/discussion and will be before the "Farewell, Feet" which is the closing remarks given by the chairperson.

"Because of the Master's Feet" worksheets for study session 3

Jesus, as our example, loved us/God so deeply that He:

1. "C"- _____

   "But the angel said to her,' Do not be afraid, Mary, you have found favor with God. You will be with child and give birth to a son, and you are to give him the name Jesus." (Luke 1:30–31 NIV).

   *He stepped into His sandals and set the example for how we should _____.

2. "R"- _____

   "Very early in the morning, while it was still dark, Jesus got up, left the house and went off to a solitary place, where he prayed." (Mark 1:35 NIV).

   "But Jesus often withdrew to lonely places and prayed." (Luke 5:16 NIV).

   *His sandals stopped moving among others as He prayed, showing us the importance of spending time

   _____.

3. "O"- _____

   "Jesus went throughout Galilee, teaching in their synagogues, preaching the good news of the kingdom, and healing every disease and sickness among the people." (Matthew 4:23 NIV).

   "He told the crowd to sit down on the ground. When

he had taken the seven loaves and given thanks, he broke them and gave them to his disciples to set before the people, and they did so. They had a few small fish as well; he gave thanks for them also and told the disciples to distribute them. The people ate and were satisfied..." (Mark 8:6–8 NIV).

Jesus was _____ the crowd.

*He showed us how to move our sandals quickly to _____.

4. "S"-_____

"...just as the Son of Man did not come to be served, but to serve..." (Matthew 20:28 NIV).

"After that, he poured water into a basin and began to wash his disciples' feet, drying them with the towel that was wrapped around him." (John 13:5 NIV).

"Now that I, your Lord and Teacher, have washed your feet, you also should wash one another's feet. I have set you an example that you should do as I have done for you. I tell you the truth, no servant is greater than his master, nor is a messenger greater than the one who sent him. Now that you know these things, you will be blessed if you do them." (John 13:14–17 NIV).

*Even though His own feet were tired and His sandals were dusty, He took the time to serve the disciples by taking care of their feet.

5. "S"-_____

"...and the blood of Jesus, his son, purifies us from all sin." (1 John 1:7 NIV).

"If we confess our sins, he is faithful and just and will forgive us our sins and purify us from all unrighteousness." (1 John 1:9 NIV).

*He took off His sandals to willingly be

_____ for _____.

Imagine the pain...!

What are you willing to do for Him?

"My command is this: Love each other as I have loved you. Greater love has no one than this, that he lay down his life for his friends." (John 15:12–13 NIV).

Thomas said, "...Unless I see the nail marks in his hands and put my finger where the nails were, and put my hand into his side, I will not believe it." (John 20:25 NIV).

"A week later, Jesus said to Thomas, "...Put your finger here; see my hands. Reach out your hand and put it into my side. Stop doubting and believe." (John 20:27 NIV).

*The nail prints were proof to Thomas that Jesus was Himself. What proof are you showing to others that you love Christ?

"This is to my Father's glory, that you bear much fruit, showing yourselves to be my disciples," (John 15:8 NIV).

"Because of the Master's Feet"
teaching notes:

Props and displays: a slipper, a flip-flop, a tennis shoe, a hiking boot, a high-heel shoe, a penny loafer, a flat shoe, a cleat, nine shoe boxes, four small signs, scotch tape, a man's sandals, a wooden cross about four feet tall that could be made out of plywood, a dark sheet to cover the cross, a hammer, and something made of metal that could be struck with a hammer to produce a loud, clanging noise.

Set-up: Have half of the shoes and shoeboxes on the right side of your speaking area and the other shoes and shoeboxes on the left side, except for the sandals. Place each shoe on a shoebox lid covering a shoebox that has been placed on the ground either vertically or horizontally. On the shoeboxes holding a shoe, tape a small sign to four of them as follows: slipper- a "Resting" sign; flip-flop-a "Thanking" sign; tennis shoe-a "Serving" sign; and hiking boot-a "Climbing" sign. (The other shoes will not have signs on their boxes, but they will be among the boxes with signs.) Cover the wooden cross with a sheet and prop it against the wall that is behind you while you are speaking. Have a volunteer prepared to clang the hammer against a metal object at the appropriate time while out of sight. Come not wearing, but carrying a man's sandals in a shoebox.

(Wear whatever shoe you feel comfortable wearing while speaking. Tennis shoes would be appropriate since you're still serving).

Special instructions: Be sure to read the scriptures where it is noted in the notes to support what is being said. Also, when giving answers to the fill-in-the-blanks, give enough time for the participants to fill in their answers before continuing to speak.

Introduction

*Have someone else open the session with prayer before you come forward to speak.

Speaker: "I come carrying the shoes that represent Jesus." (Open the box, take the sandals out of the box, show the shoes to the ladies in the room, and place them on the lid of the box as you place both the lid and the box on the ground near your stand.) "I am not worthy to wear the shoes that represent Jesus. As John the Baptist said in part of Mark 1:7, He is '...more powerful than I, the thongs of whose sandals I am not worthy to stoop down and untie.' (Mark 1:7 NIV)

"In this final session, we will see how Jesus' life is our example to follow. We will see how His feet took Him to the throne of God to share what was on His heart, how He walked from place to place to meet the needs of others so unselfishly, how He served His own friends, and how He sacrificed His own life at Calvary for each and everyone of us."

Study session

"Jesus' most loving gift to us while He was still here on earth as a human was giving His life for us at the cross. So, let's begin filling in this acrostic of the "cross."

Jesus, as our example, loved us/God so much that He:

1. "C"-(Came to earth as man).

   "But the angel said to her, 'Do not be afraid, Mary, you have found favor with God. You will be with child and give birth to a son, and you are to give him the name, Jesus.' (Luke 1:30–31 NIV).

   "He came and experienced the things that we, as humans, have to face and deal with in this lifetime. He was willing to 'walk in our shoes' to prove His love for us. As Ruler and King of all, He didn't have to, but to be our precious Savior, He chose to. He loved us/God so much, He came to earth to live as a loving example and to lovingly die for us."

*He stepped into His sandals and set the example for how we should (live).

2. "R"- (Related intimately with the Father). Here are only a few examples of the times He spent alone with the Lord:

    'Very early in the morning, while it was still dark, Jesus got up, left the house and went off to a solitary place, where he prayed.' (Mark 1:35 NIV)

    'But Jesus often withdrew to lonely places and prayed.' (Luke 5:16 NIV).

"Notice that it was important to Him to spend time with the Lord by Himself. The Lord did not intend for us to spend time with Him only during a worship service at church. Although these times are important, nothing can take the place of being with Him alone as you share and listen to Him. If Jesus Who was perfect did this, then, we who are imperfect people should be convicted to spend time with Him daily on a regular basis. To truly know God and know what He desires for your life, you have to spend time with Him."

*His sandals stopped moving among others as He prayed, showing us the importance of spending time (alone with God).

3. "O"- (Opened His eyes to the immediate needs of others). As He saw needs of others, He provided for them. Look at the verses below and fill in the blanks that follow each

verse, showing how Jesus met the needs of others. These examples represent only a few of the many times He met the needs of others." Give the group time to answer for both verses, then, have someone read the verses and give her answers after each verse.

Volunteer: "Jesus went throughout Galilee, teaching in their synagogues, preaching the good news of the kingdom, and healing every disease and sickness among the people." (Matthew 4:23 NIV). Answer: "Jesus went throughout Galilee, (teaching), (preaching), and (healing)."

Volunteer: "He told the crowd to sit down on the ground. When he had taken the seven loaves and given thanks, he broke them and gave them to his disciples to set before the people, and they did so. They had a few small fish as well; he gave thanks for them also and told the disciples to distribute them. The people ate and were satisfied…" (Mark 8:6–8 NIV). Answer: "Jesus was (feeding) the crowd."

Speaker: "In fact, Jesus fed about four thousand men with this small amount of food and even had leftovers. Jesus is always so wonderful in meeting needs in a bigger and better way than expected. His ways are never common. The brush-stroke of God across the canvas of life is always magnificent!

*He showed us how to move our sandals quickly to (meet the needs of others).

4. "S"-(Served with an eternal value).

   'Just as the Son of Man did not come to be served, but to serve, and to give his life as a ransom for many.' (Matthew 20:28 NIV).

   'After that he poured water into a basin and began to wash

his disciples' feet, drying them with the towel that was wrapped around him.' (John 13:5 NIV).

'Now that I, your Lord and Teacher, have washed your feet, you also should wash one another's feet. I have set you an example that you should do as I have done for you. I tell you the truth, no servant is greater than his master, nor is a messenger greater than the one who sent him. Now that you know these things, you will be blessed if you do them.' (John 13:14–17).

"In the verse from Matthew, we see that He was speaking of the ultimate gift of service, dying on the cross for us. This He would choose to do for all mankind. In the verses in John 13, we see how Jesus served His own disciples by washing their feet, and through this act, He showed all of us the example of how we should serve each other. If the majestic King of the universe can stoop down on bended knee to wash the dirty feet of many, then we have no excuse to not serve with all our hearts in whatever way He calls us to serve."

*Even though His own feet were tired and His sandals were dusty, He took the time to (serve) the disciples by taking care of their feet.

"Jesus' greatest act of service, which Jesus spoke of in the verse just mentioned in Matthew 20:28 is described under the last letter, "S." He showed us His love for us the most when He…

5. "S"-(Sacrificed Himself). Jesus sacrificed His own body through an excruciatingly, painful death. He allowed him-

self to be nailed to a cross in order to save us from our sins, if only we confess them.

'…and the blood of Jesus, his son, purifies us from all sin'. (1 John 1:7 NIV).

'If we confess our sins, he is faithful and just and will forgive us our sins and purify us from all unrighteousness.' (1 John 1: 9 NIV).

*He took off His sandals to willingly be (crucified) for (us).

"Listen to me closely, and close your eyes as we try to imagine the pain He felt in the events that preceded His experience at the cross": (Pause after each statement).

- Imagine that the hour of your death is approaching and your friends are sleeping while you agonize in prayer.
- Imagine that one of your own betrayed you for money and is turning you over to the 'authorities' to be murdered.
- Imagine being arrested and sentenced to death for no crime.
- Imagine being disowned by one of your closest friends three times.
- Imagine being spit on and beaten for no just cause.
- Imagine a crowd knowing all about you, but they choose to release a murderous criminal instead of you, who has done nothing wrong.
- Imagine the feeling of rejection you're experiencing.

"Now, with your eyes still closed, let's go to the site of the cross:

- Imagine being laid on an old cross as soldiers drive nails into your hands and feet.

- Imagine hanging on a cross for hours until your last breath.
- Imagine the pain!

Now, open your eyes and look up here at me. You can only *imagine* these things because you didn't have to experience them. But Jesus did!"

(Uncover the cross and have the lights dimmed, if possible. Make sure the person who is responsible for using the hammer is in place and ready. Then, pick up the sandals and hold them in your hands as you begin to speak)

"These sandals represent Christ's service to mankind, but He took them off so that He could give the greatest act of service possible, His life." (Take the sandals and place them at the foot of the cross.) "As they placed Him on the cross, He knew the pain He would endure and He chose to stay on the cross for us. Each time the hammer struck those sharp nails that pierced His righteous hands and feet, He felt the weight of the sins of the world."

"Listen now, and think of your own sins being nailed to the cross as He continually suffered for you and me. Put yourself at the foot of the cross and imagine the pain! (Have someone out of view hit the piece of metal with the hammer to make a very loud clanging sound. Instruct her to hit it 12 times and to pause after each strike. Afterwards, have the lights returned to regular strength.)

"Jesus showed He loved us by giving no excuse when He willingly hung on that old, rugged cross. He proved what He was willing to do for us. What are you willing to do for Him?" (Pause.)

"Look at the next verse:

'My command is this: Love each other as I have loved you.

Greater love has no one than this, that he lay down his life for his friends.' (John 15:12–13 NIV).

"What kind of sacrifices have you made for God and for your friends? Have you 'stepped out of your comfort zone' to show your love for Christ?

"After Jesus had appeared to the disciples after His resurrection, Thomas did not believe Jesus had appeared because He was not there to see Jesus. Thomas said,

'...Unless I see the nail marks in his hands and put my finger where the nails were, and put my hand into his side, I will not believe it.' (John 20:25 NIV)

"A week later Jesus appeared to the disciples again and said to Thomas,

'...Put your finger here; see my hands. Reach out your hand and put it into my side. Stop doubting and believe.' (John 20:27 NIV).

"The nail prints proved to Thomas that Jesus was Himself. What actions do you take to prove that you love Christ? Can you tell by your works that you love God?

'This is to my Father's glory, that you bear much fruit, showing yourselves to be my disciples.' (John 15:8 NIV)."

Closing

"This area around me displays many types of shoes, and several of the shoes represent a certain action you can choose to take in your walk with the Lord. Hopefully, you have tried each of these pairs of shoes on and feel comfortable about putting them on again and again. But God can use all types of feet, Christians, to do many types of services for Him. These other shoes represent whatever God has placed on your heart to do for Him in service. Yes, the tennis shoe was our model for service, but you can wear high heels to serve when you sing the Sunday morning solo in the worship service or perhaps, wear one of these other shoes to be a Christian example at a sporting event or in your everyday life. As you look at the cross and His empty shoes, be reminded that God loves you and desires for you to walk with Him wherever you go."

"The music leader is going to play some music, and while she does, if you need to come to the cross, kneel, and pray about whatever the Lord has placed on your heart today, please do so. He is waiting for you to commit to be 'at His feet' daily and to serve 'as His feet' to each other and to a world that needs His love." (The music begins.)

Prayer at the cross

*Let the women respond. You may want to be the first to kneel at the cross or you may want to kneel and pray with them. Let the Spirit lead the rest of this session as He knows the hearts of the women and what they need better than anyone. Be in prayer for the ladies during this important time. After at least three or four minutes, you may ask the music leader to stop playing the music if everyone has stopped coming forward. Just be sure you don't cut this time too short.

* Ask if anyone would like to share what's been placed on her heart today. After everyone that wanted to share has shared, ask for prayer requests from the group. Tell the ladies they can record the requests from the group on the "prayer requests" page provided in their books. After the prayer requests have been made, pray aloud for all of the ladies and the requests that were made. Then, turn the program over to the chairperson for the final remarks.

Checklist for the Speaker/Study session leader

Before the retreat

- ❑ Pray.
- ❑ Read, study, and take notes on all of your material in your section.
- ❑ Become familiar with your study session worksheets and what you're supposed to say in reference to them.
- ❑ Make note cards. (Optional)
- ❑ Practice your delivery while emphasizing enthusiasm and eye contact.
- ❑ Gather or make all props and use them while practicing your delivery.
- ❑ Contact any volunteers and give them specific instructions about their duties, and tell them what session(s) they will be needed.
- ❑ Help with the leaders' early set-up the day of the retreat. (See if you can have a stand to use for your materials while you are speaking.)
- ❑ Take all materials and props to the retreat setting.

At the retreat

- ❑ Come wearing slippers!
- ❑ Have all props and displays in place for each study session before the study session begins, if possible.
- ❑ Focus on God and deliver each study session with His power. (Let Him speak through you)

After the retreat

- ❑ Help with the clean up of the retreat setting.
- ❑ Go home and rest!
- ❑ Write hand-written thank-you notes to any volunteers who helped you fulfill your obligations.

Dear Speaker/Study session leader,

Thank you so much for agreeing to accept this very important leadership position. I'm sure you touched hearts for His Kingdom as you motivated the ladies to sit "at His feet" and to serve "as His feet!" I pray that God richly blessed you through this experience, and that He will continue to use you to convict others into action when it comes to daily loving and doing for Jesus.

> Thank you for serving "as His feet,"
> Cheris, the retreat writer

Addendum

Participant guides are available by contacting the author at cherisgaston@yahoo.com and including "Slippers– Participant's Guide" in your subject line. Further information will be provided upon request. Please allow 4 weeks to receive the guides.

CPSIA information can be obtained at www.ICGtesting.com
Printed in the USA
BVOW06s1323170216

437071BV00011B/73/P